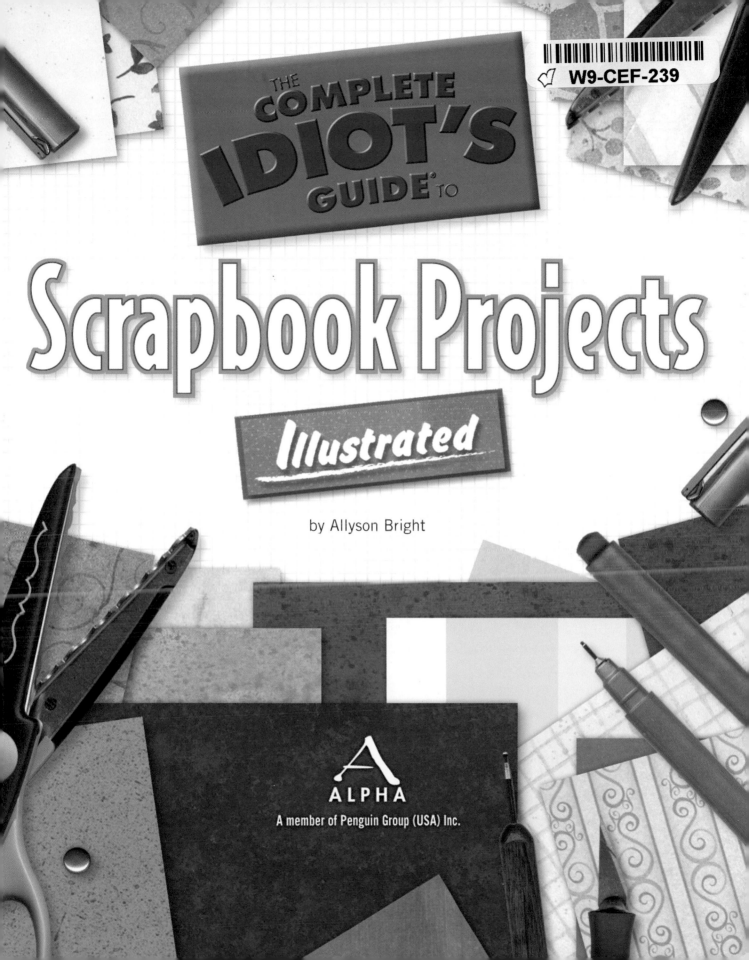

THE COMPLETE IDIOT'S GUIDE TO

Scrapbook Projects

Illustrated

by Allyson Bright

A
ALPHA

A member of Penguin Group (USA) Inc.

For Grandma and Grandpa, who have always believed I was meant to write and create. This is for you.

ALPHA BOOKS

Published by the Penguin Group

Penguin Group (USA) Inc., 375 Hudson Street, New York, New York 10014, U.S.A.

Penguin Group (Canada), 10 Alcorn Avenue, Toronto, Ontario, Canada M4V 3B2 (a division of Pearson Penguin Canada Inc.)

Penguin Books Ltd, 80 Strand, London WC2R 0RL, England

Penguin Ireland, 25 St Stephen's Green, Dublin 2, Ireland (a division of Penguin Books Ltd)

Penguin Group (Australia), 250 Camberwell Road, Camberwell, Victoria 3124, Australia (a division of Pearson Australia Group Pty Ltd)

Penguin Books India Pvt Ltd, 11 Community Centre, Panchsheel Park, New Delhi—10 017, India

Penguin Group (NZ), cnr Airborne and Rosedale Roads, Albany, Auckland 1310, New Zealand (a division of Pearson New Zealand Ltd)

Penguin Books (South Africa) (Pty) Ltd, 24 Sturdee Avenue, Rosebank, Johannesburg 2196, South Africa

Penguin Books Ltd, Registered Offices: 80 Strand, London WC2R 0RL, England

Copyright © 2006 by Allyson Bright

International Standard Book Number: 1-59257-504-8
Library of Congress Catalog Card Number: 2006903504

08 07 06   8 7 6 5 4 3 2 1

Interpretation of the printing code: The rightmost number of the first series of numbers is the year of the book's printing; the rightmost number of the second series of numbers is the number of the book's printing. For example, a printing code of 06-1 shows that the first printing occurred in 2006.

Printed in the United States of America

Note: This publication contains the opinions and ideas of its author. It is intended to provide helpful and informative material on the subject matter covered. It is sold with the understanding that the author and publisher are not engaged in rendering professional services in the book. If the reader requires personal assistance or advice, a competent professional should be consulted.

The author and publisher specifically disclaim any responsibility for any liability, loss, or risk, personal or otherwise, which is incurred as a consequence, directly or indirectly, of the use and application of any of the contents of this book.

Most Alpha books are available at special quantity discounts for bulk purchases for sales promotions, premiums, fund-raising, or educational use. Special books, or book excerpts, can also be created to fit specific needs.

For details, write: Special Markets, Alpha Books, 375 Hudson Street, New York, NY 10014.

Publisher	**Marie Butler-Knight**
Editorial Director	**Mike Sanders**
Managing Editor	**Billy Fields**
Director of Marketing	**Dawn Werk**
Executive Editor	**Randy Ladenheim-Gil**
Senior Development Editor	**Christy Wagner**
Senior Production Editor	**Janette Lynn**
Copy Editor	**Molly Schaller**
Book Designer	**Kurt Owens**
Proofreading	**Mary Hunt**

Contents at a Glance

PART 4

Celebrating Yourself

PART 5

Sharing the Love

Appendixes

Contents

Foreword

I'm a mother to four busy boys, and I'm doing my best to teach them the value of work. On Saturday mornings, each boy gets a clipboard with a checklist of chores to do. Before I send them off, I always say, "Okay, got everything need? Any questions?" To their mumbled groans, I then respond, "Great! No excuses then—just a job well done!"

My first thought after reading *The Complete Idiot's Guide to Scrapbook Projects Illustrated* was *Wow!* There are no excuses anymore. This book is clear, concise, and comprehensive in its treatment of what is now one of America's most popular pastimes. In a high-tech, fast-paced, globally connected world, scrapbooking is a chance to step back, reflect, and feel gratitude for one of life's simplest pleasures: happy memories.

In this book, Allyson Bright writes with a conversational tone and offers so much personal insight, you'll be jotting ideas right and left of the pages and projects you want to create. Beautiful full-color illustrations and helpful information boxes sprinkled on nearly every page will make you feel as though Allyson is at your side, anticipating your next question, sharing her expertise.

One of my favorite ideas—and really I should say *solutions*—is the project in Chapter 5, "Happy Holidays: Celebrating Your Annual Traditions." Here, Allyson proves that creating a meaningful keepsake can be as easy as bringing together a few of the highlights from years of family celebrations. From my experience interacting with and teaching scrapbookers over the years, one of the biggest hurdles to getting started—and staying motivated—is the idea that we need to scrapbook *all* the pictures that fill *all* the boxes in *all* the closets. That's simply not true. Remember this: any time you pair a memory with a photograph, you are scrapbooking, and every time you make a page or complete a project, you are adding another chapter to a unique and wonderful story—yours.

You can do this. With *The Complete Idiot's Guide to Scrapbook Projects Illustrated,* you've got everything you need! Questions? I didn't think so.

Here's to a job well done!

Stacy Julian
Founding editor, *Simple Scrapbooks* magazine

Introduction

Yes, you can scrapbook. I can't begin to count the number of times I've talked with someone about my love of scrapbooking, only to hear them say in response, "I could never do that." But yes, you can.

I think the fear of scrapbooking stems from several different places. Some people are worried that if they start now, they'll be obligated to create albums for the 20+ years of photographs currently sitting under their beds in shoeboxes. Others feel like they couldn't possibly be artistic enough to create an album worth sharing. Still other people simply feel that they don't have the time or money to invest in the hobby. Are you struggling with any of these worries? Fear no more. You can scrapbook.

I'm going to let you in on a little secret: I don't consider myself a highly artistic person. Although I've always enjoyed writing and creating things, somehow my drawings of people always ended up looking more like awkwardly formed giraffes than a group of friends. And although scrapbookers often become artists in their own right, that's not the real driving force behind this hobby.

You're no idiot. You picked up this book because you want to learn how to preserve your photographs and memories. You want to make them tangible so you can share them with others. And that's what scrapbooking is truly about. It's not about how much time you spent creating your pages or what color combination you chose. It's about remembering how joyful you were when you found out your niece was born, how in love you felt when your boyfriend proposed, and how overwhelmingly proud you were when you finally graduated from college. Scrapbooking is about the details.

No matter how much time or money you want to invest, this book helps you capture the details of your life and preserve them for future generations. Scrapbooking isn't about pressure. Don't worry about the need to scrapbook the years of photos behind you, or succumb to the pressure of creating an artistic masterpiece the first time you cut a sheet of paper. Focus on the moment. Your child's birth. Your father's birthday. Your brother's basketball game. Focus on the details.

Take the time to grab on to a memory, a favorite moment from your past. Now imagine if you had a way to re-live that moment as often as you wanted and even to share to feeling of that moment with another person. That is the joy of scrapbooking. So grab on to your memories. It's time to get started. Yes, you *can* scrapbook.

HOW TO USE THIS BOOK

This book is for you, to help you preserve the moments and memories from your own life. If you're completely new to the world of scrapbooking, I recommend starting at the beginning. By the end of the first chapter, you'll already be creating scrapbook pages. And you'll also find that you don't have to be a world-class artist to do it!

Want to create an entire album right away? Jump in wherever you see fit. The projects in this book are all suitable for beginners. If you come across a skill or term you're not familiar with, simply flip back to the first part of the book for clarification. Some of the simplest projects in this book can be found in Chapters 5 and 7.

No matter where you choose to start reading and creating, remember that this book is designed to help you preserve your own memories, which might be different from mine. Feel free to adapt each project to meet your own needs. Change the theme slightly, or simply trade out one product for another. Step-by-step instructions are provided for each project to help you create it easily. But don't be afraid to break away from the rules if inspiration should strike.

This book is organized into four parts:

Part 1, "Ready, Set, Scrap!" introduces you to scrapbooking and provides you with real knowledge and tools to start creating pages and projects immediately. If you're brand new to the world of scrapbooking, I recommend spending a considerable amount of time in this part to get accustomed to the hobby, the lingo, and the tools required of our trade.

Part 2, "Commemorating Your Experiences," helps you create fantastic albums and scrapbook pages centered around the most significant events of your life: your school years, your child's growth, holiday celebrations, and more. If you want to work through a large pile of photographs, these projects are for you.

Part 3, "Celebrating Your Relationships," offers a number of unique projects honoring the most important people in your life—from your best friend to your parents and back again. These albums make wonderful gift items and can also serve as a way of honoring someone who is no longer in your life.

Part 4, "Sharing the Love," is for the addicted scrapbooker. If you're not one yet, never fear. Work through a few of the projects in other parts of this book, and you'll likely soon be joining the ranks of those who consider scrapbooking not just a hobby, but a lifestyle. These projects enable you to share the joy of your hobby with others by creating beautiful art with others and also by creating art to share with others.

Finally, you'll find a set of appendixes. One offers you a selection of fill-in-the-blank worksheets that will help you as you create the projects in this book. You'll also find a complete list of all the products used to make every single page and project shown in this book, identified by manufacturer when applicable. If you see something you like on a project, this will help you identify the item so you can purchase it for yourself. The remaining appendixes are designed to help you if you have questions while reading or wish to be directed to an outside source for more information about a particular product or technique.

EXTRAS

Throughout this book, you'll find four different information boxes that provide you with help or extra information as you're reading:

PICTURE THIS

I share fun tips and tricks to enhance your projects in these boxes.

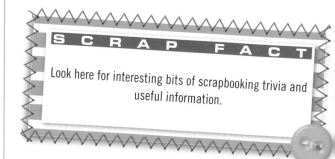

S C R A P   F A C T

Look here for interesting bits of scrapbooking trivia and useful information.

PAPER **C**UTS

Check these boxes for warnings as you're working on projects. They can help you avoid frustrating mistakes.

SCRAP SPEAK

These boxes offer simple definitions of scrapbooking terms.

ACKNOWLEDGMENTS

I am so thankful I received the opportunity to write this book. Scrapbooking and writing are my two real passions in life, so being given the chance to combine them has truly been a dream come true. There are so many people without which this book would not have been possible. I would like to express true gratitude to the following individuals:

Randy Ladenheim-Gil, Christy Wagner, and the rest of the team at Alpha Books. I have been privileged to work with you. Thank you so much for helping me create the best book possible.

Jacky Sach of BookEnds, LLC. Without you, this simply would not have been possible. Thank you for showing me the ropes of the publishing industry and for your constant guidance and support.

Andrea Steed of Scrapjazz.com, for providing me with my first opportunity to write about scrapbooking. I love being a part of the Scrapjazz team, and I look forward to many years to come. Thank you for your guidance and friendship. It has been a true pleasure.

Kris Ortale and all the employees at Memories on Fifth in Coralville, Iowa. Teaching at your store has been such fun! I would also like to thank the many individuals who attend my classes on a regular basis. Thank you for trying out many of these projects before they went to press.

The many companies who donated both their industry knowledge and product to help this book be a success: 7gypsies, Anna Griffin, Arctic Frog, BasicGrey, Chatterbox, Crafty Secrets, Creative Impressions, Daisy D's, Duncan Enterprises, EK Success, Flair Designs, Heidi Swapp, Junkitz, Karen Foster Design, KI Memories, Making Memories, Melissa Frances, O'Scrap, Provo Craft, QuickKutz, Scrapworks, Spellbinders, Stampington & Company, Venus Industries, Wordsworth, Wrights, and Xyron.

My talented team of contributing artists. Thank you for sharing your stories and art with me. It has been such a delight to partake in life's ups and downs with you. I would like to give an additional thank you to Rachael Giallongo, Michelle Van Etten, Alecia Ackerman Grimm, Angie Hagist, Alexis Hardy, and Leah Blanco Williams, as well as young artists Ashley Orr and Jenny Barnes, for sharing their time and talent.

Daniel J. Meyer for providing fantastic photographs of products and completed projects.

To all the families who allowed me to scrapbook their photographs and stories. Thank you for trusting me with your memories. Thanks to Abby and Tucker, for allowing me to share in their athletic successes. And to the kids who provide me with so many smiles (along with many hilarious photographs)—Amber, Ashley, Annamarie, Ben, and Addie—I am so blessed to know you.

To my own family: Daniel, Mom, Dad, Carrie, Matt, and Anna. Not only have you endured many hours of my constant scrapbook-based chatter, but you've allowed me to share your faces and our stories with the world. I am so grateful to have such an amazing support system.

TRADEMARKS

All terms mentioned in this book that are known to be or are suspected of being trademarks or service marks have been appropriately capitalized. Alpha Books and Penguin Group (USA) Inc. cannot attest to the accuracy of this information. Use of a term in this book should not be regarded as affecting the validity of any trademark or service mark.

All project supply lists were believed to be complete and accurate at time of publication. If you believe an error or omission has been made, please contact the publisher so corrections can be made in future editions.

7gypsies is a registered trademark of 7gypsies LP.

Aleene's is a registered trademark of Duncan Enterprises.

Bobbin Ribbon is a registered trademark of Morex Corp.

Marvy is a registered trademark of Uchida of America Corp.

Tulip is a registered trademark of Duncan Enterprises.

Select sticker designs © 1998 Mrs. Grossman's Paper Co.

Part 1

Ready, Set, Scrap!

So you've seen the scrapbook pages of others and want to create your own. Or perhaps someone gave you a gift of a few basic supplies and now you're not sure where to begin. In Part 1, I introduce the hobby of scrapbooking to you. You'll learn the basics, from album selection to paper types. We'll look at how to use your computer to enhance your scrapbooks and a few basic photography techniques, and we'll even explore some new and trendy techniques. Finally, I teach you some basic design principles you'll be able to quickly and easily apply to any of your future creations.

Rest assured, after reading this part and trying out a few of these techniques, you'll be able to create truly artistic pages and albums like a pro—even if you've never scrapbooked before.

WHATCHA lookin at?

I can't stop looking at this picture of Madeline. Maybe it is her eyes, her cute

DRIVE MY CA

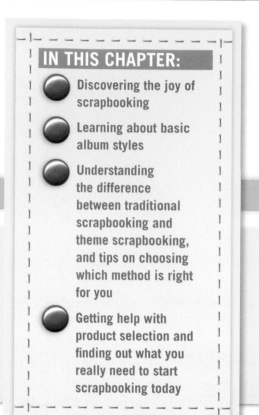

IN THIS CHAPTER:

- Discovering the joy of scrapbooking

- Learning about basic album styles

- Understanding the difference between traditional scrapbooking and theme scrapbooking, and tips on choosing which method is right for you

- Getting help with product selection and finding out what you really need to start scrapbooking today

memories of

SANTA

Chapter 1

Scrapbooking Basics

Welcome to the fantastic world of scrapbooking! Before you begin any new hobby, it's generally a good idea to learn the basics. This chapter helps you discover the reasons you should scrapbook, shows you the different ways to do it, and gives you the basic skills you need to begin. Let's go!

WHY SCRAPBOOK? AND HOW?

Chances are, you picked up this book for a reason—you want to scrapbook! But why? And what exactly is *scrapbooking,* anyway? Maybe you just want to get a few photos into a basic album and would like to try something a little different from a standard photo album. Or perhaps you're already an accomplished artisan and are simply looking for a new method of self-expression. Whatever brings you to the table, scrapbooking might just be the perfect hobby for you.

SCRAP SPEAK

Scrapbooking is the act of taking photographs and combining them with specialty papers, accents, and journaling to create a customized photograph album.

Why do you want to scrap? Knowing and understanding the reason you want to scrapbook will help you throughout every step of the process. Do any of the following statements describe you?

- "I've seen other people's scrapbooks, and I think they're cute. I want to try creating one of my own."

- "I'm tired of keeping all my photographs stored in shoeboxes. I want to share them with the people I care about."

- "A friend gave me some scrapbooking supplies as a gift, but I have no idea how to use them."

- "I've loved creating art since I was a child, and I think scrapbooking would be a fun way for me to use my artistic ability."

- "I'm not looking to create a masterpiece. I just want to get my photographs into a nice-looking album for my child."

As you can see, there are all sorts of reasons to begin scrapbooking. No matter where your desire lies, this book can help you gain the skills you need to create beautiful and lasting albums. From the simple to the elegant, you can create heirloom-quality albums that matter.

CHOOSING AN APPROACH

There are two basic ways to approach scrapbooking. Generally, scrapbook pages and projects can be grouped into two basic categories: *traditional scrapbooking* and *theme scrapbooking.*

Choosing the way you'd like to scrapbook can be essential in helping you approach your projects. Many artists choose to scrap in both ways, depending on what best fits the project at hand. Which method is best for you? Let's take a closer look and find out.

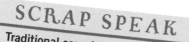

SCRAP SPEAK

Traditional scrapbooking is a method of scrapbooking in which pages are created and displayed in chronological order, generally with one page devoted to each major event occurring in a calendar year.

Theme scrapbooking is an approach to scrapbooking that focuses on relationships, events, and emotions with equal emphasis. Pages are created and displayed in an order chosen by the artist and do not have to be arranged chronologically.

Take a moment to ponder these questions:

- **Do you want to create a record of every event that occurs in each year of your life?**

- **Do you want to create multiple albums, similar in nature, to share with your each of your children, and for them to take with them when they leave home?**

- **Do you want all your scrapbooks to be the same size?**

- **Do you wish to create only one or two albums each year?**

Now, answer these questions:

- **Do you want to record emotions and relationships in your scrapbooks in addition to events?**

- **Do you like the idea of having multiple scrapbooks in an assortment of sizes and designs, some spanning the course of a single event and others spanning decades?**

- **Do you want to create scrapbook pages reflecting on your personality and childhood?**

- **Do you hope that each project you create will be new and different from the last?**

If you answered "yes" to many of the first questions, then traditional scrapbooking is for you. If you found yourself answering "yes" to many of the second questions, you're a theme scrapbooker. Did you answer "yes" to most of the previous questions? A combination approach is probably best for you. Still can't decide? Take a look at the following two scrapbook pages.

This holiday layout was done from a traditional scrapbooking perspective. The layout documents a single holiday and includes the date.

This layout, done from a themed perspective, combines photographs from many years to create an emotionally charged layout.

Which layout do you like better? Both layouts have a lot to offer both the artist and the viewer.

Regardless of the approach you choose to take when creating your scrapbook pages, it's time to get started. Most of the album projects in this book take a themed approach, but we'll look at many ways to create pages for your chronological scrapbooks as well.

S C R A P   F A C T

Stacy Julian, founding editor of *Simple Scrapbooks* magazine, pioneered the theme scrapbooking movement when she published her 2000 book, *Simple Scrapbooks*.

STOCKING UP

Getting started is one of the hardest parts of scrapbooking. You have to select your tools, album, and your first set of products. Many new scrapbookers make the mistake of either skipping one of the necessities or simply buying too much. The key is to keep things simple. When getting started, purchase only what you absolutely need. You can always add to your supply collection later.

PHOTOGRAPHS

Photographs are the backbone of any well-created scrapbook. As an aspiring scrapbook artist, you likely have plenty of these to work with already. However, when you begin to choose your photographs for your first scrapbook projects, keep the following tips in mind. Your scrapping experience is then sure to be a happy one.

- Work with copies of your original photographs rather than the originals themselves. Your first scrapbook page is not the place to cut up the one and only photograph of your Great Aunt Louise.

- Having a system for organizing your photographs, either print or digital, is essential. Search online for free photo organization software programs, such as *Picasa*, to aid you in this task. Visit www.picasa.com to download this great program.

- The photographs are the spotlight of your album. Don't be afraid to make enlargements to let your photos truly shine.

WHATCHA lookin at?

I can't stop looking at this picture of Madeline. Maybe it is her eyes, her cute smile, her chubby little fingers smudging the clean window. Maybe it is the rosy cheeks, or the cute little polka dot onesie. Maybe it is the fact that she is pulling up on everything. Maybe it is that cute button nose, or those gorgeous thighs. I got it! I am lookin' at it ALL!

march 04

My cute little Maddie

This scrapbook page features an enlarged photograph spotlighting this adorable baby girl. The result is just perfect.

(Layout by Monica Schoenemann)

ALBUMS

Regardless of which approach—traditional or themed—you've decided to take when scrapbooking, your pages are going to need a home. Placing your finished pages in album allows them to be shared and enjoyed with others and also keeps them safe from harm.

Selecting your first album is probably one of the most important purchasing decisions you'll have to make. But don't worry—I walk you through it.

Albums come in many shapes, sizes, and binding styles. For your first scrapbook album, I recommend purchasing either a 12×12-inch or 8½×11-inch album. Focus on creating your early scrapbook pages all in the same size and adding them to your album as you complete them.

Selecting the type of binding you'd like your album to have is one of the hardest parts of choosing an album. Many choices are available, and it's easy to feel overwhelmed by the options. Some of the most common album bindings are *post-bound, 3-ring,* and *spiral.*

- **A post-bound album is a scrapbook that's bound using a system of posts and screws. Completed pages are placed in page protectors. Post-bound albums are expandable and are generally considered the most attractive type of album.**

- **3-ring albums are one of the most versatile albums on the market today. Completed pages are placed in page protectors, which are then stored in the album's ring system. 8½×11-inch office binders make an affordable choice for the scrapper on the budget. 3-ring albums are not expandable.**

- **Much like an everyday school notebook, spiral-bound albums consist of several blank pages bound together into a single album. These albums are not expandable and do not contain page protectors.**

These two beautiful albums are just a sampling of the choices you'll find when selecting your first scrapbook album.

A good choice for your first album is a post-bound or 3-ring album. These albums enable you to protect and display your pages in style. They are also very forgiving if you want to remove or change a page later on, or if you're still determining the order in which you'd like to display your completed scrapbook pages.

THE PERFECT CUT

Cutting tools are must in the world of scrapbooking. There are many, many options available to you, but only two tools are absolutely necessary.

First, be sure you own a good pair of scissors, and dedicate them solely to your scrapbooking. Micro-tipped scissors work especially well for small, precision cutting.

PAPER CUTS

Using your scrapbook scissors to cut other materials might dull the blades and render them less effective over time. Keep one pair of scissors solely for your scrapbook projects.

Second, a high-quality paper trimmer is essential. Trimmers generally come in two standard sizes, full-length and mini. A full-length paper trimmer enables you to cut a straight edge across your entire length of paper, up to 12 inches. The mini version is great for cropping photographs and smaller items. Many scrapbookers choose to keep both sizes on hand, but a single full-size trimmer should be all you need for the projects you'll accomplish in this book.

These beautiful papers from Daisy D's, KI Memories, and Chatterbox are just a few of the coordinating collections you can find at your local scrapbooking store.

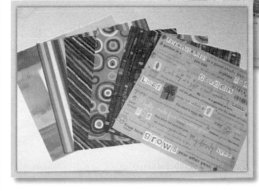

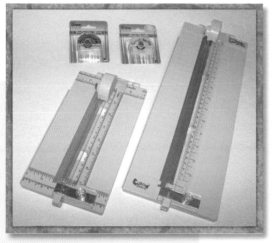

These paper trimmers from the Cutterpede collection by EK Success are a fantastic choice for your paper crafting projects.

PAPERS

Now that you have your photographs, album, and cutting tools selected, you're probably eager to choose the papers you'd like to create with.

When it comes to the world of scrapbooking, many people—including me—believe you can simply never have enough paper. And major companies have responded to this way of thinking by offering more patterned papers, cardstock papers, and specialty papers than you could ever imagine. Start by purchasing a small assortment of papers. You can add to your collection later as your skills and style develop.

PICTURE THIS

While you're still a beginner to the world of scrapbooking, consider purchasing paper in bulk packs that offer a wide variety of designs and textures. These paper collections offer a great value to the beginning scrapbooker. Or check your local scrapbook store for coordinating paper collections from many different manufacturers.

Office supply and stationery stores also offer papers you might like to include in your scrapbooks. Although many of these papers are suitable for your albums, some are not considered scrapbook-safe due to their acid content. For more information on what's safe to use in your scrapbooks and what's not, see Chapter 3.

STICKING IT ALL TOGETHER

You've finally got all the pieces of the scrapbook page. Now all you need is a great adhesive to hold everything together. Numerous adhesive choices are available to the scrapbook artist.

Scrapbook adhesive comes in two basic forms: *dry* and *wet.* It's generally best to start by purchasing one of each. Scrapbook adhesives aren't often cheap, so if possible, it's a good idea to try a few out before investing in one. Many scrapbook stores allow you to try a product before you purchase it. Simply ask if there is a sample available so you can see how it works.

SCRAP SPEAK

Dry adhesive is an adhesive that is dry to the touch, yet tacky. It does not run, is applied like a tape, and is set immediately upon application. Dry adhesive is best for adhering paper to paper.

Wet adhesive is a liquid-based adhesive that requires additional time to dry before it's set. Wet adhesive is best for applying other materials (such as metal, plastic, and wood) directly to paper.

Perhaps the best form of dry adhesive is the tape runner. This handy dispenser enables you to apply tape directly to your project without worrying about sticky fingers or gooey messes. To apply, simply expose the tip of the tape runner, press it on your paper, and pull toward you. The tape is dispensed directly on to your project. When purchasing a tape runner, pay careful attention to both the length and width of the adhesive being dispensed. This directly impacts how long the adhesive will last, as well as the cost of the adhesive.

SCRAP FACT

Dry adhesives come in both permanent and removable forms. If you're unsure about a project while you're creating it, consider using a removable adhesive so you can make changes to your design after you've glued it down.

Owning a wet adhesive is also important for new scrapbookers. This enables you to adhere smaller items and accents to your pages. When selecting a liquid adhesive, choose one that advertises a "strong bond." Also be sure the glue you select is marketed for scrapbookers and is photo safe and archival quality.

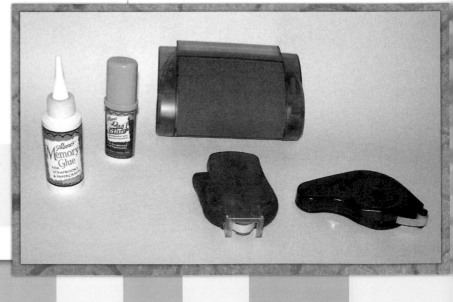

These adhesives by EK Success, Xyron, and Aleene's are well formulated and deliver a strong—and safe—bond for your scrapbook projects.

THE "WRITE" DETAILS

The final basic tool you need to begin scrapbooking is at least one high-quality pen. Pens are used to add dates, journaling, and other important details to your scrapbook pages. It's important that the pens you use are archival quality and photo safe. Look for a pen that advertises these qualities on the packaging. Scrapbook-friendly pens should have permanent, pigment-based ink.

Pens come in a wide variety of styles, colors, and ink types. From metallic pens to bright writers, brush tips to calligraphy pens, you want to be sure the pens you select enable you to add details to your pages that will stand the test of time.

At first, you might be tempted to purchase a large number of pens, but keep things simple. A single, black pen is all you truly need to get started. Select a few others if you want and then allow your collection to grow as your interest and skills expand.

This assortment of pens comes from the Zig collection by EK Success. Zig pens are known for their quality and permanence.

CREATING YOUR FIRST PAGE

Believe it or not, you now have all the tools you need to create your first scrapbook page. Although the aisles upon aisles of fun stickers, die cuts, and other scrapbooking treats are likely tempting you already, remember that the most important parts of a scrapbook page are your photographs and memories.

Prepare to create your first page by gathering a collection of photos you'd like to work with. Next, select a paper or two to match. Pull out your basic tools, and you're ready to begin.

STEP ONE: CROPPING AND MATTING

Cropping is one of the most basic things you'll need to do as a scrapbook artist. If your photographs contain ugly background elements or you simply want to make them smaller, you'll want to begin the process of creating your page by cropping them down to the size you'd like to work with.

Following the directions that came with your paper trimmer, align your photograph to the edge of the trimmer, noticing where the cut will be made. Carefully pull the trimmer blade toward you, and you've made your first cut! Repeat this process until all your photographs are the size you'd like to work with.

Next, you might want to create a *mat* for one or more of the photographs on your page.

To create a photo mat, simply measure a piece of decorative paper slightly larger than your photograph. Trim your paper to size, and adhere it to the back of your photo.

Take some time to determine how you'd like your photos and text to appear on your page. When you've made up your mind, adhere your photographs to your page.

STEP TWO: ADDING TEXT

Every scrapbook page contains two important pieces of text: the page's title, and the *journaling.*

Every page should have a title. This lets the page's viewer know what's going on in the photographs and provides a hint toward the type of information contained in the page's journaling. In general, a page's title should be short and to the

point and should appear larger on the page than the journaling text.

Basic scrapbook journaling is simple and easy to create. If you're creating a traditional scrapbook page, this might consist solely of the date the photographs were taken. If the page you are designing is more themed in nature, you might want to add some additional information.

You can add text to your scrapbook pages in many ways. You can use your computer or any one of a number of specialty scrapbooking products designed solely for that purpose. For now, though, just grab a pen or two and jot down the information by hand. You now have your very first scrapbook page.

One of my earliest scrapbook pages, this layout uses only cardstock and a pair of pens to mirror the fun and lighthearted nature of my best friend as she appears in these photos.

After you've made your first page, you're ready to dive in to all the hobby has to offer. Just a few small additions can make a page go from fairly plain to pretty fabulous!

THE LEAST YOU NEED TO KNOW

- Scrapbooking is a fun and enjoyable hobby.

- Traditional scrapbooking approaches events and photographs from a chronological standpoint. Theme scrapbooking allows for a more emotion-based approach.

- When selecting products for your first few scrapbook pages, remember to purchase only what is absolutely necessary. You can always buy more later.

- All you need to get started in scrapbooking is a handful of photographs, an album, a few basic cutting tools, papers, a pen, and some adhesive. Then you're ready to go!

- Creating your first scrapbook page is quick, fun, and easy.

Adding just two elements—a patterned paper mat and cut-out letters—to your basic supplies makes this page truly fun to look at.

IN THIS CHAPTER:

- Building a foundation for your scrapbook page

- Adding the necessary elements to make your page complete

- Journaling techniques to ensure your pages contain all the necessary details

- Working with layout sketches, design templates, and product kits to make page design quick and easy

- Gaining confidence in your color selections

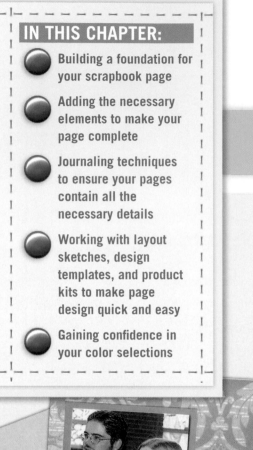

Anna's Baptism
aug. 21, 2004

Chapter **2**

Putting It All Together: The Elements of Design

Let's face it: the average scrapbooker is not a graphic designer. But just because you might not have a college degree in fine art, who's to say you can't create truly stunning scrapbook pages?

The art of scrapbook design is nothing more than putting together the pieces of the puzzle: photographs, product, and journaling. It's just that simple!

BASIC ELEMENTS

Every scrapbook page or project contains a few basic elements. Understanding each of these elements and how to use them effectively is the most important part of the design process. When you understand the way everything fits together, you'll design beautiful scrapbook pages each and every time you sit down to create.

WORKING WITH PHOTOGRAPHS

As you learned in Chapter 1, photographs are the backbone of a scrapbook page. They are, after all, the reason you decided to scrapbook in the first place, right? Scrapbooking is about preserving photographs and the memories that go with them.

When creating a scrapbook page, it's important to keep the emphasis of the page on your photograph or memory. For this reason, it's important to establish a *focal point* on your scrapbook page.

SCRAP SPEAK

A **focal point** is the strongest element on a scrapbook page, and the place on the page to which your eye is naturally drawn.

As you sit down to create your page, take a minute to ask yourself: *What do I want to be the most important thing on this page? Which photo is the most important?* When you know the answer to these questions, you can proceed with the design of your page.

One of the easiest ways to establish a photograph as the focal point on your page is to use an enlarged version of the photograph you want to highlight.

This beautiful layout not only uses a photo enlargement, but the artist went one step further and created a silhouette by cutting out the background of the primary photograph. The emphasis on this layout is exactly where it belongs.

(Layout by Tanya-Marie Pocino, owner, Outrageous Daisy)

If you find yourself in a situation in which you simply don't have the room to use an enlargement (or you simply don't want to), there are many other ways to establish a focal point on your scrapbook pages. Try one of these easy techniques:

- **Mat your focal point photo in a contrasting color so it stands out from the rest of your page.**

- **Crop your focal point photo into a special shape or cut out the background elements to create a silhouette.**

- **Use an arrow or other design element on your page to "point" to the focal point photo.**

After you've established the focal point of your layout, it's time to begin thinking about the journaling you'd like to include on your page.

THE ALL-IMPORTANT WORDS

I know so many scrapbookers who hate to include journaling on their scrapbook pages. They simply don't want to take the time to write down the facts behind the photographs, or they think they have to be a skilled writer to create effective journaling. These thoughts simply aren't true. Journaling on your scrapbook pages is one of the most important elements you can include.

Scrapbook journaling tells us the who, what, when, why, and where of your photographs. If you're scrapbooking a family holiday celebration, you might only need to include the date to create an accurate record of the event. But what if you're creating a page celebrating your son's recent baseball game? Or your daughter's high school prom?

I first started scrapbooking while I was a student at the University of Iowa. I created page after page celebrating my friendships and the random, silly things we spent doing together. I never once took the time to add journaling. Looking back on those pages now, some of that information is lost to me. I simply can't remember what that guy in the background's name was. Or who was her roommate? The information is gone, and I can never get it

back. The best way to keep this from happening to you is to take the time to write down the important event you're commemorating. If it's worthy of a scrapbook page, it's worthy of journaling.

Still don't feel up to writing? Try one of these techniques to create a unique layout:

- **Start with a simple list. Who, what, when, where, why. You can even label each item.**

- **Take the perspective of a news reporter and provide journaling from a point of view other than your own.**

- **Practice interview journaling. Not sure what your child was thinking when you snapped that photo? Ask him and then write it down.**

- **Record the same event from the perspective of everyone present in your photographs.**

PICTURE THIS

Try keeping a small notebook in your purse or backpack. As you snap photos, jot down the facts of the location, time, event, etc. as well as your emotions. When you scrapbook your photos later, your journaling is already complete!

This layout captures the daily life experiences and perspectives of every member of the household. The result is a fun and unique way to look at what must be going on in the minds of the people shown.

(Layout by Heidi M. Deck

This touching layout showcases an interview between mother and daughter, talking about everything from her child's feelings about being 5 years old to her message for her father stationed overseas.

(Layout by Teresa Olier)

The journaling on scrapbook pages doesn't need to simply be an afterthought. Sometimes, all it takes is a date hidden in the corner of a page. But other times, your photos have an important story to tell. Don't let it become lost.

PUTTING IT TOGETHER

As you can see, photographs and text create the basis for all scrapbook pages. When you combine these elements with papers and products, you have the perfect recipe for a beautifully finished page. There are many different ways to assemble a scrapbook page. Now that we've built on what you learned in Chapter 1, it's time to put this new knowledge to the test.

CAN'T SOMEONE ELSE DO IT?

We all want beautiful scrapbook pages. We look through the latest issue of *Memory Makers* or another popular scrapbooking magazine and think *I could never do that*. That's just simply not the case. Many manufacturers have released products that have the design work done for you. All you have to do is add your photographs and text, and you've got a completed page ready to add to your album.

One of my favorite new product releases in this area is a coordinating line of papers and accents by Anna Griffin. The predesigned layout pages are ready for you to add your photographs and journaling. Ready-made photo mats and three-dimensional accents fit perfectly on each page, giving you a stunning layout in a minimum amount of time.

These products designed by Anna Griffin work together to help you create a beautiful scrapbook page without a lot of effort or time.

To create a layout using this system, follow these simple steps:

1. Begin by selecting a blank layout page.

2. Add your photographs and journaling.

3. Finish your layout by adding frames and layered cardstock stickers. Feel free to offset the frames slightly to add interest.

Using a system such as this enables you to create incredibly quick and beautiful layouts. "Anna's Baptism" took slightly less than 10 minutes to complete.

PICTURE THIS

When using coordinated kits, many times you may have extra paper and embellishment scraps after you've completed your layout. Try using these smaller pieces to create a greeting card or two (see Chapter 18 for several ideas), or use them as smaller accent pieces on another scrapbook page.

WORKING FROM KITS

Anna Griffin is currently one of the only companies producing such an easy system to work with, but many manufacturers do offer coordinating lines of paper and embellishments to make your page creating a snap.

Your background papers might not be predesigned to provide the easiest layout assembly, but you can create fantastic pages by following the same basic steps you used to create the previous layout. Simply begin by choosing where you'd like to place your photographs. Then create mats, frames, and background accents using additional patterned papers. Finish off your layout by adding a tag or other decorative element.

This layout was created using KI Memories' "Evergreen" collection of patterned papers and tags. The result is a beautifully coordinated layout.

Creating scrapbook pages from coordinated paper collections is a quick, easy, and fun way to scrapbook. Many manufacturers sell and package their coordinated collections as individual items, so you can pick and choose which items you'd like to buy.

If you prefer to purchase an entire kit at a time, consider joining a monthly direct-mail scrapbooking club. Monthly clubs offer preselected coordinating kits that are shipped directly to your door for the same price each month. (These prices are often highly discounted off the suggested retail price.) Some clubs offer a kit choice each month, while others select the products for you. Be sure to research the policies of each club thoroughly before you join.

PICTURE THIS

If you're interested in joining a monthly scrapbooking club, check out the following popular club websites:

Scraptivity, www.scraptivity.com
Kit 'n' Kaboodles, www.knkclub.com
Mosh Posh, www.mosh-posh.com
Club Scrap, www.clubscrap.com
Coordinates Collections, www.coordinatescollections.com

Another way to get fantastic kits without joining a monthly direct-mail club is to ask for them at your local store. Many stores will put together kits for you at no additional cost. Or consider taking a class at a local store, where you'll likely receive a complete kit as well as guided instruction for a specific project.

DESIGNING FROM SKETCHES

You're certainly moving right along, aren't you? You've created a page using just the basics. You've learned about creating an effective focal point on your layouts, and you've mastered the art of

creating with coordinated products. Now it's time to begin selecting your own products and creating your own designs.

One tool many scrapbook artists use to design their pages is the *layout sketch.*

SCRAP SPEAK

A **layout sketch** is a layout outline indicating the placement of photographs, journaling, and other page elements.

One of the key benefits of working with layout sketches is the freedom they offer. Although the basic structure of the layout is given, you are able to make your own final placement choices. Some layout sketches are quite detailed, and others are much more abstract. Consider the following layout:

This beautiful page is simply and elegantly designed—and it's quite a bit of fun as well.

(Layout by Rachael Giallongo)

By understanding the basic design elements of this layout, it's easy to see what makes it so great. Take another look at this page, this time in sketch form:

photo	photo
	photo

title

Rachael's design consists of four blocks, each containing an element of its own.

This page contains a few more design elements to add interest. The reflective journaling and ribbon are particularly nice touches.

(Layout by Kate Schaefer)

By examining the layout sketch, you are able to see how to create a layout of your very own. Check out these two additional layouts, also designed with a four-block emphasis.

This layout uses a simple four-block background to create a dramatic setting for this adorable photo.

It's easy to see how a similar basic design can produce several different looks. When you find a page design you love, learn to look at it as a sketch. Then, feel free to adapt the design into a layout of your very own.

We'll use layout sketches throughout this book to create albums, design pages, and more. If you'd like to find more layout sketches to use on your own, try searching online. Many scrapbooking websites, such as Scrapjazz.com, offer layout sketches and challenges.

PAPER CUTS

Remember that scrapbook page designs are copyrighted works of original art. If you decide to adapt someone else's design, be sure to give that person credit if you choose to post the design in an online gallery or submit it to a magazine.

COLOR CONFIDENCE

One of the last major areas to discuss in scrapbook design is the use and selection of color. Color choice is an essential decision in the world of scrapbooking. You wouldn't create a St. Patrick's day page using orange and black, would you? I didn't think so.

When selecting a color scheme for a scrapbook page or project, it's important to think about the tone you want to put into the page. Knowing what type of mood you want to convey is crucial to selecting the products for your design. Before you begin, ask yourself the following questions:

- **What do I want this layout to convey? Am I trying to express excitement? Grief? Joy?**

- **Are there any important colors I need to use because of the photos I've selected (i.e., holiday colors, school's colors)?**

- **Do I want this page to have a calming effect or an invigorating one?**

Color choice is perhaps the one thing that determines the final voice and feel of your layout. Take a look at the next layout.

This bright, fun page perfectly conveys the subject's sunny personality.

(Layout by Becky Lynn Teichmiller)

It's easy to see how the color choices in this layout provide an energetic and upbeat feeling. If this layout had been done in a combination of red and brown, the result would have been quite different.

Next, let's examine this page:

This gorgeous page uses a combination of pinks and browns to create the perfect mood. The colors and products chosen are a fantastic match for these introspective photographs.

(Layout by Tanya-Marie Pocino, owner, Outrageous Daisy)

This page has a much different feel from the last one, but again, the colors create the perfect feeling. What if this layout had been done in sunny yellow and bright red? The warm, deep feeling you get while looking at it would be completely gone. Similarly, if "Always Laugh" had been designed in soft pastels, the layout would then feel like it was missing something.

Also, take a look at the photographs themselves. When choosing your supplies, be sure to they're in colors that coordinate with your photos. If your photos showcase your daughter in her pink and blue Halloween costume, don't be afraid to pass over the traditional orange and black color scheme on your scrapbook page.

THE LEAST YOU NEED TO KNOW

- Use an enlarged or accented photograph to create a strong focal point on your scrapbook pages. This ensures that your page's emphasis remains on your photographs and memories.

- Journaling is an essential element of any scrapbook page, even when you record only a few small details.

- Working with page kits, coordinated products, and predesigned papers helps you create balanced and beautiful pages with minimal time and effort.

- Layout sketches can help you design the structure of your project while giving you freedom to make your own creative decisions.

- Selecting a color scheme that effectively creates the mood you desire for your scrapbook page is an important part of the design process and can be completed quickly by simply asking yourself a few quick questions.

IN THIS CHAPTER:

- Adding memorabilia and children's artwork to your scrapbook pages

- Using accents and embellishments to further the theme of your scrapbook page

- Understanding and choosing scrapbooking's advanced tools

- Creating scrapbook pages with texture, dimension, and shine by using not-so-ordinary scrapbooking and craft supplies

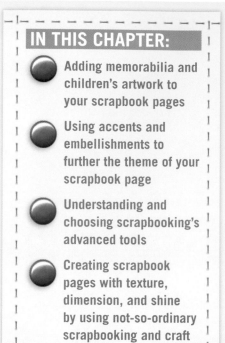

Chapter 3

Beyond the Basics: Creating Pages That Stand Out

You might have noticed that after completing some of your first scrapbook pages, it felt like something was missing. Perhaps you saw a beautiful sticker at your local scrapbook store and wanted to add it to your page. Or maybe your page felt too flat or too plain. The end of these problems is near. Let's discover ways to create scrapbook pages that truly stand out.

ADDING TO YOUR PAGES

Your scrapbook page has all the basics—photography, journaling, even some beautiful patterned paper. But something just isn't quite right. You need to find the perfect *accent,* or *embellishment* to add to your layout.

SCRAP SPEAK

A scrapbook **accent,** or **embellishment,** is a predesigned add-on for a page, often a sticker or die-cut shape.

Accents and embellishments come in all shapes and sizes. From dimensional fabric shapes, photo corners, and metal frames, to long border stickers, you can generally find the perfect accent for your layout simply by browsing your local scrapbook store.

Using Accents and Embellishments

Embellishments can often provide the perfect finishing touch for a scrapbook page. They add interest and flair and help communicate the message of your scrapbook page. Embellishments and accents come in many forms. Here are some of my favorites:

- **Photo corners (especially metal photo corners)**

- **Small frames**

- **Alphabet stickers and die-cut shapes**

- **Licensed sticker collections for your favorite brands, such as Disney, Harley-Davidson, NASCAR, Coca-Cola, and more**

- **Precut tags**

- **Paper flowers**

As you can see, you have many options to choose from when it comes to adding to your scrapbook pages.

This beautiful layout would be very plain without the addition of a few key elements. Notice the metal frame, the fabric flowers and wedding clothes, and the small heart-shaped brads that surround the photo.

(Layout by Kate Schaefer)

Preserving Memorabilia

When it comes to finding the perfect product to accent your layout, sometimes you don't have to look far—you might already have it in your home. Perhaps you'd like to include a ticket stub from a recent sporting event, newspaper clipping, or even a recent drawing from your child. Never fear: there are ways to include these items in your scrapbook without harming the original while keeping the rest of your scrapbook photo-friendly.

First, determine whether or not you'd like to use the actual item on your scrapbook page. Will a color copy suffice? If so, that's your best option. Take your item to a local copy store for copying. Be sure you request acid-free paper and archival quality ink. This ensures that you get a copy that will last for years to come. Creating color copies also works well for items that are slightly larger than the surface you're working on, as you are free to reduce or enlarge the original item according to your page design.

PICTURE THIS

Techno-savvy? Save time and money by making your own archival copies at home using a scanner and printing with high-quality ink on acid-free photo paper.

This layout beautifully highlights the art of a child and preserves the drawing for generations to come.

(Layout by Teresa Olier)

If you really want to use the actual item on your scrapbook page, a few options are available to you. First, consider working with a product such as Archival Mist or Make It Acid-Free. These products,

when sprayed evenly on any paper item, create an acid-free buffer, making the item safe to include in your scrapbook.

PAPER CUTS

Remember that memorabilia items often contain quite a bit of acid. Even when treated, it's best to mount these items on acid-free cardstock and be sure no edge of the paper is touching your photographs. This ensures that your photographs will stay free of acid and other harmful toxins.

A final way to include memorabilia on your pages is to photograph it. After all, you can't easily mount a favorite outfit, sports medal, or trophy to a piece of paper!

Place the item to be photographed against a solid-colored background. Then, simply point and shoot to take a photograph of the item you love. You can now include this photograph as part of a special scrapbook page.

This fun page celebrates my favorite childhood friend, Rocky the Raccoon.

PICTURE THIS

Don't have a solid-colored wall in your home to photograph against? Hang a solid-color bed sheet from the top of your wall to the floor, and you have an instant photography studio.

CREATIVE IMAGES AND TEXT

By now, you've learned the ins and outs of adding flair to your scrapbook pages with stickers or including a special keepsake on the page. But to truly take your scrapbooking to the next level, you're going to want to step it up a bit. There are many easy ways to add creative text and images to your pages and albums.

Using the Computer

The personal computer is one of the greatest resources available to scrapbook artists. With the nearly unlimited number of fonts and typefaces available, creating beautiful lettering is only a single print away. Clip art and stock photo sites also offer many options to the scrapbook artist. Try browsing the Internet to find images and fonts that will best complement the design you're working on. (Check out Appendix D for some online browsing starting points.)

After you've found the perfect font for your journaling or the perfect image for your layout, it's time to print it and add it to your page. It's important to note that each printer works differently. Be sure to follow the instructions provided by your printer's manufacturer to ensure an accurate print.

By now, you might have a key question: *How can I use my standard computer printer with*

12×12-inch paper? This question leaves many scrapbookers stumped, and even reluctant to use their computer to add journaling or text to their pages. However, using your computer to achieve great printed results on 12×12-inch paper is quick and easy. Just follow these simple steps:

1. **Cut your paper to 8½ inches on one side, leaving the other side 12 inches long. Set aside the remaining piece.**

2. **Using the page layout menu in your word processing program, set the size of your paper to 8½×12 inches. Set margins of your choice.**

PICTURE THIS

If your program does not allow custom paper sizes, select "legal" size paper. Add an additional 2 inches to the right margin of your paper to allow for the difference in paper size.

3. **Feed your patterned paper into the printer and print.**

4. **Add your printed page to your layout, using adhesive to rejoin the two sections of paper together. By covering the seam with ribbon, photographs, or a creative border element, you'll totally hide the fact that your paper was printed with an "ordinary" computer.**

This layout was printed using a standard printer. By adding a border of photographs across the bottom of the pages, the cut line is completely hidden.

Stamps and Rub-Ons

When it comes to adding text and images to your scrapbook art, two fantastic tools shouldn't be overlooked. Unlike stickers, both create a totally borderless design on a scrapbook page. And unlike the computer, design can be added anywhere on your page, without having to cut or alter the paper in any way.

First, let's take a look at stamps. Stamps come in many forms: rubber, foam, and acrylic. All three are fun to use and create excellent results when used on scrapbook pages.

These stamps by Making Memories, EK Success, Wordsworth, and Stampington & Company are just a few of the many choices available to scrapbookers.

There are two parts to a stamp. First is the stamp image itself. The image is etched into rubber or acrylic or is created out of foam. Second is the handle of the stamp. Most common stamps are mounted onto a wood or foam block that features the design of the stamp. Some stamps feature a clear plastic handle that provides the artist full creative control over their design.

Using a stamp is simple. Just follow these steps:

1. **Press the image repeatedly into an ink pad. There's no need to rock the stamp into the ink or rub it across the surface of the pad. A few presses ensures that the stamp is inked smoothly.**

2. **After your stamp is inked, take a quick look at the design to ensure the ink covers all areas of the image. If so, you're ready to stamp.**

3. **Press the stamp *firmly* on the paper where you would like the image to appear. Do not rub or rock the stamp while pressing.**

4. **Lift the stamp *straight up* off the paper. Do not lift the stamp at an angle.**

You now have a beautifully stamped design.

Almost as easy to use as stamps are *rub-on transfer images*, or rub-ons. Although they are a relatively new trend in the scrapbooking world, rub-ons have been available for quite some time.

SCRAP FACT

Stamps have been around for centuries. They first appeared as wax seals. Hot, melted wax was used to seal envelopes containing important correspondence. Then, using a special stamp, the sender would press his initial or crest into wax before it had time to harden. Historically important people, such as kings, would always seal their envelopes in this way.

SCRAP SPEAK

Rub-on transfer images are letters or images set on a sheet of translucent specialty paper. When this paper is placed over another sheet of paper and rubbed firmly, the image transfers to the new paper without leaving a seam or any additional marks.

Rub-ons are a perfect addition to your scrapbook page. Like stamps, they can be used anywhere on a layout. One of the key benefits of rub-ons is their clean and professional appearance. In addition, many scrapbookers enjoy the fact that rub-ons are available in myriad colors that don't work well in other mediums. This is especially true of white rub-ons.

This layout uses a combination of rub-ons and rubber stamps to create the title and corner calligraphy image.

Home Cutting Systems

Perhaps one of the greatest innovations in the scrapbooking world is the home cutting system. In the early days of scrapbooking, small paper punches were about the only thing available. If you wanted a larger die-cut shape, or a set of letters, you had to travel to a local store that offered die-cutting services. Fortunately, this is no longer the case. A variety of cutting systems has been introduced to the industry. Each is unique in its own way and has quite a bit to offer every scrapbook artist, regardless of skill level.

One of the hardest things to do as a scrapbook artist is know which cutting system is best for you. There are many factors to consider when purchasing a system, including cost, portability, storage options, design preferences, and more. Let's take a look at some of the most popular systems on the market and their key advantages.

PICTURE THIS

Want to try before you buy? Many local scrapbook stores have at least one of these cutting systems available in their classroom. Ask store personnel for a demonstration and trial. Often, the choice can simply be a matter of what feels best in your hands.

COLUZZLE

The Coluzzle system, produced by Provo Craft, was one of the first home cutting systems introduced to the craft market. It remains popular today.

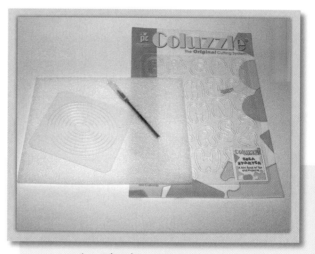

The Coluzzle cutting system includes a soft cutting mat, a swivel-tipped knife, and a series of templates.

Templates are the most important part of the Coluzzle system. Each template has a series of grooves, increasing in size, that create a specific shape or design. You simply place your paper on the cutting mat and position the clear template over your paper, lining up the groove of your choice with your project. Then you just trace around the desired shape's groove with the Coluzzle swivel knife. Lift up the template, and you now have a perfectly cut shape.

Key advantages of the Coluzzle system:

- **Cost.** Because the Coluzzle cutting system does not require the purchase of a machine, it is significantly cheaper than all the other major systems.

- **Template versatility.** Each template, with the exception of alphabet templates, offers many size choices for each shape.

- **Portability.** The system is extremely portable. You can easily fit the knife, mat, and an entire collection of templates into a 9×12-inch envelope or carry them in a standard tote bag.

Limitations of the Coluzzle system:

- **Limited designs.** Because of the trace-and-cut nature of the system, only a limited number of template designs are available to choose from.

- **Blade replacement.** The knife's blade needs to be replaced after heavy use.

All the circles on this adorable layout were cut using the Coluzzle system.

(Layout by Angie Hagist)

When cutting with the Coluzzle, be sure to hold the knife steady and pull it at an even pace to avoid slightly crooked edges.

SQUEEZE BY QUICKUTZ

Often considered the trendiest system of the bunch, the Squeeze hand tool offers an extremely portable choice for the scrapbook artist.

The QuicKutz die-cutting system includes the Squeeze hand tool and an assortment of small, wafer-thin dies.

Like the rest of the systems we'll be looking at, the QuicKutz system is die based. Rather than using a template to trace and cut your design, the images exist on small dies. To cut the design, you apply pressure to the die.

To use the Squeeze hand tool, simply select a die and place it into the mouth of the hand tool. The flat side of the die should line up flat against the magnetic plate inside the hand tool. Place your paper on top of the die and then simply squeeze the handles together and remove your die-cut shape.

Key advantages of the QuicKutz system:

- **Portability and storage.** The handle is small enough to travel anywhere. The dies store nicely in small storage binders so your entire collection of dies can fit in just a few inches of space.

- **Availability and quality of designs.** QuicKutz offers one of the largest design libraries available for any system. You'll find basic geometric shapes, intricate two-piece designs, elaborate cityscapes, and more. QuicKutz is constantly introducing new shapes and fonts, keeping with the latest trends in the scrapbooking industry.

- **Range of accessories.** QuicKutz manufactures a wide variety of accessories that are the perfect complement to your hand tool, including totes, exclusive paper strips, storage binders, and more.

- **Ability to add texture.** Using new texture dies, QuicKutz users can add an embossed texture of your choice to its shapes. Popular designs include small circles, a basket weave texture, and sparkles.

Limitations of the QuicKutz system:

- **Size.** All QuicKutz dies are the same size. Creating larger designs with the system requires that you piece two or more shapes together.

- **Pressure.** Some users find that the hand tool requires a great deal of pressure to ensure an even cut.

SIZZIX

The Sizzix die-cutting system is a fantastic choice for artists who want to have the ability to create large, simple designs with their home cutting system.

The Sizzix system consists of the Sizzix machine, as well as steel-rule dies crafted from heavy-duty plastic with foam padding.

Sizzix dies are larger and have more padding than QuicKutz dies, making them easier to cut with. To use, simply place your paper on the Sizzix

cutting pad and line up your die on top. Slide the cutting pad into machine, and pull down the handle. Remove your shape and enjoy!

Key advantages of the Sizzix system:

- **Ease of use.** The Sizzix is arguably the easiest system to use. Children as young as 8 years old should be able to use the system on their own, with appropriate supervision.

- **Variety of die sizes.** The Sizzix library includes dies in all shapes and sizes, including larger shapes perfect for many projects.

- **Cutting ability.** The Sizzix system can easily cut through many different materials, including paper, craft foam, fabric, rubber, magnetic sheets, and more. This makes the Sizzix a fabulous tool for all your crafting needs, not just scrapbooking and paper crafts.

- **Adaptability.** The manufacturers of Sizzix work hard to keep their system compatible with current trends. Recent additions to the line include embossing plates as well as shape dies that both cut and score for folding, enabling the user to create fantastic cards, mini albums, and more.

Limitations of the Sizzix system:

- **Storage options.** Because the dies are so large, they take up a lot of space in storage. Sizzix offers a rotating tower designed to hold dies, but if you have a large collection, it will fill up fast.

- **Weight.** The Sizzix is significantly heavier than most other systems, making it a poor choice for easy transport.

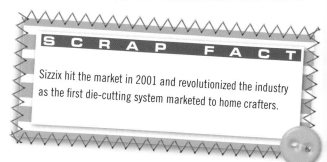

SCRAP FACT

Sizzix hit the market in 2001 and revolutionized the industry as the first die-cutting system marketed to home crafters.

THE SIDEKICK

The Sidekick is manufactured by the makers of the Sizzix machine, and the two systems are designed to work together.

The Sidekick system includes a small, portable machine; two cutting mats; and thin, steel-rule dies.

To use the Sidekick, you simply create a die "sandwich," which you then run through the machine. Start by laying a cutting pad on the table. Add the die, face up. Place your paper on top of the die, lining it up as you desire. Place the second cutting mat on top, finishing off the die-and-paper "sandwich." Grasp the sandwich firmly and feed it through the Sidekick machine, rotating the handle toward you. Pull the sandwich out on the other side of the machine, and you'll be left with a perfectly cut shape.

Key advantages of the Sidekick system:

- **Portability. The Sidekick machine is lightweight and can easily travel with you to a scrapbook event or a friend's home.**

- **Range of dies available. Sidekick dies, called Sizzlits, are available in a variety of fonts and shape choices.**

- **Adaptability. Sidekick dies can also be cut in the Sizzix system. QuicKutz and other brands of thin dies can be cut in the Sidekick system. (Note: both of these actions require the separate purchase of an adaptor.)**

Limitations of the Sidekick system:

- **Size. Only one size die works with the Sidekick system, not allowing for larger shapes or designs. The Sidekick does offer long border-shaped designs, but these still come only in one width.**

THE WIZARD

The last system we'll take a look at is the Wizard embossing and die-cutting system, manufactured by Spellbinders. This system is the perfect choice for the crafter who wants a tool that will do it all.

The Wizard system includes the embossing and die-cutting machine, Spellbinders-style embossing and cutting dies, and a variety of cutting and embossing mats, which are fed through the machine.

The Wizard machine is certainly the most complicated of all of the machines, but it's also the most versatile. Like the Sidekick, the Wizard works by creating sandwiches of cutting mats, dies, and paper, which are then fed through the machine. The orientation of these sandwiches varies greatly depending on what you're trying to do at the time.

The Wizard machine is both a cutting system and an embossing system. Each die can be used to cut, to emboss, and as a stencil. As a result, final shapes cut with the Wizard machine have both shape and texture, which is unique to the Wizard system. Consult the machine's user manual to assemble your die and paper sandwich and feed it through the machine.

Key advantages of the Wizard system:

- **Adaptability. Dies from almost any manufacturer can be used in the Wizard machine without the purchase of a separate adaptor. This is the only machine with this capability.**

- **Multiple functions. In addition to its built-in cutting and embossing functions, the Wizard can do numerous other tasks. A few examples include embossing with metal charms and rubber stamps, flattening bottle caps and clay, creating photo transfers, and more. Visit www.jenlowedesigns. com/lucymcgoo.htm to download the unofficial Wizard manual, which provides a complete guide to all sorts of creative uses for the Wizard machine.**

- **Size and weight. For a machine of its capability, the Wizard lacks the bulk and weight of similar machines.**

Limitations of the Wizard system:

- **Learning curve. Although it doesn't affect the actual capability of the system, the user learning curve for this system is somewhat difficult. Don't expect novice or younger users to be able to pick up the basics very quickly.**

All these home cutting systems are excellent choices for the beginning or experienced crafter. Some new crafters might not like the idea of the initial investment, but it's a purchase that pays for itself in the long run. Remember that although purchasing stickers and premade embellishments might seem cheaper, dies have unlimited uses. You might be able to get text for only two or three scrapbook pages from one package of stickers. With a cutting system, you can create text and images for thousands of pages and projects.

This beautiful layout features perfectly matched die-cut elements from the Wizard's collection of dies.

(Layout by Michelle Van Etten)

TERRIFIC TEXTURE

Perhaps what separates a good scrapbook page from a great scrapbook page is the use of texture and dimension. Applying just a touch of texture makes the elements on your layout stand apart from one another and creates a fantastic overall effect.

Distressing

One of the easiest ways to instantly add texture to a project is to *distress* your project.

There are many ways to add a distressed look to your scrapbook projects. Try one of these fun techniques:

- **Crumple your cardstock or paper into a ball and then flatten it out again.**

- **Tear the edge of your paper instead of cutting it.**

- **Using an inkpad, brush ink around the edges of your paper. This not only provides an aged look, but also helps your element truly stand out.**

- **Use sandpaper to remove just a bit of color from your project, creating a well-worn look.**

Chipboard

The use of *chipboard* on scrapbook pages is currently one of the industry's hottest trends. You're likely used to seeing chipboard. It's commonly found as the back cover to spiral notebooks, and even in your scrapbook supplies, generally to provide a safe and sturdy backing when shipping beautiful patterned papers. Recently, however, chipboard has taken a front and center role in the scrapbooking world.

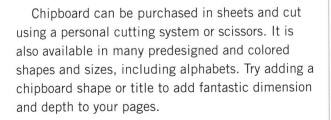

SCRAP SPEAK

Chipboard is a cheap, stiff, paper board made from discarded paper, usually used as backing material in packaging.

Chipboard can be purchased in sheets and cut using a personal cutting system or scissors. It is also available in many predesigned and colored shapes and sizes, including alphabets. Try adding a chipboard shape or title to add fantastic dimension and depth to your pages.

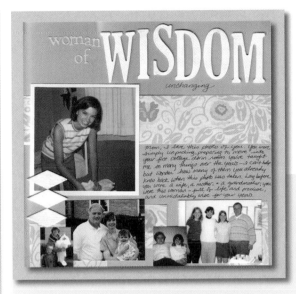

This layout features white chipboard letters as part of the title as well as a trio of chipboard diamonds painted white to add interest.

Fabric Store Finds

Many items that were once limited to fabric crafts are now finding their way onto scrapbook pages. Ribbon, silk flowers, lace, and iron-on decals are just a few. All these items create fantastic effects when added to paper.

Try creating a border or frame out of ribbon or lace. Add a flower accent to the corner of a photograph. Use iron-on letters to create the perfect dimensional page titles. These are just a few of the amazing ways fabric store finds can be used on your scrapbook pages with amazing results.

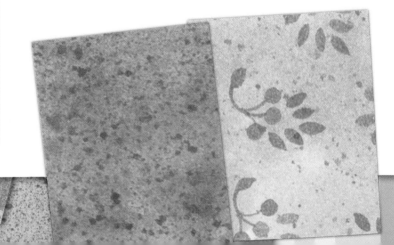

Iron-on letters create a fun title for this page.

Lace, ribbon, and flowers are just a few of the reasons this scrapbook page is so pretty.

(Layout by Michelle Van Etten)

FABULOUS COLOR AND SHINE

Another great way to create scrapbook pages that truly stand out is to make pages that have deep color and shine. Accomplishing this is quick and easy using just basic paints and dyes.

Paint

Paints aren't just for ceramics anymore; a number of paints are ideally suited for scrapbooking. The most important thing to look for when selecting a paint product is rich, opaque color. I've found that acrylic paints and fabric paints produce the best results when working with paper.

Applying paint to your scrapbook project couldn't be simpler. Squeeze a small amount of paint onto a plastic palette or other surface. Using a dry foam brush, simply dip the brush into the paint and apply it to your project. Fabric paints often have an applicator tip attached to the bottle that can also be used.

PICTURE THIS

Old compact discs make excellent paint palettes. Save them from your junk mail, use once, and then throw them away.

Try some of these uses for paint:

- **Brush a trace amount of paint around the edges of a photograph to provide contrast.**

- **Fill in a black-and-white design.**

- **Paint chipboard the color of your choice to perfectly match your project.**

- **Create a custom-colored page background.**

- **Brush a light-colored paint underneath your page title or journaling text to make it truly stand out.**

- **Use paint instead of ink when working with rubber or foam stamps.**

These specialty paints by Making Memories, Heidi Swapp, and Tulip are perfect for your next project.

This layout uses paint to create a custom striped background, with stencil accents and stamped designs to match.

(Layout by Michelle Van Etten)

Dyes

Dyes are commonly found in fabric stores, but they're no longer reserved just for fabric. Dyes are perfect for creating matched elements when paper crafting. Many manufacturers, including Making Memories, now produce dyes exclusively for paper. However, fabric dyes and color washes work equally well. And because dye was designed for fabric, elements that don't work well with paint, such as ribbon and silk flowers, work exceptionally well with dye.

This gorgeous layout features hand-dyed flowers and paper, as well as glitter, to create a beautiful overall effect.

(Layout by Michelle Van Etten)

These dyes by 7gypsies, Rainbow Rock, and Tulip are perfect for scrapbooking. The spray bottles allow for clean, easy application

Dyes are perfect for creating softer looks on scrapbook pages. Using paint provides a bold, dramatic look; the use of dye creates a softer, more even-toned feel.

Try some of the following uses for dye:

- **Create perfectly coordinating paper, tags, and die-cut shapes.**

- **Dye florals and ribbon to match your project.**

- **Use in place of ink or paint when stamping.**

THE LEAST YOU NEED TO KNOW

 Including memorabilia on your scrapbook pages is an easy and worthwhile process.

 Stamps and rub-ons are fantastic tools for adding images and text to your projects.

Home cutting systems are a fantastic choice for cutting titles and shapes for your layouts. When making a purchasing decision, be sure to consider all factors to help you determine which system is right for you.

Distressing your pages, using chipboard, and adding items from the fabric store to your pages are all great ways to add texture and depth.

 Paint and dye are excellent mediums for creating perfectly matched scrapbook pages that truly stand out.

Summer Swim Days

Commemorating Your Experiences

When you pull out your camera to take a photo, why are you doing so? Ninety-nine percent of the time, it's because something is happening that you want to remember. This is the reason to create scrapbooks celebrating your experiences.

No matter what event you want to scrapbook—a special vacation or your annual holiday traditions— I teach you how to create a unique album to commemorate even your most treasured memories. Some of these projects might seem intimidating at first, but by applying the techniques and skills you learned in Part 1, you'll have no trouble at all making these fun and easy projects. Plus, I show you some ideas for including these memories in your traditional scrapbooks as well. Whether it's your child's first year of life, a special year in school, or even your progress through a sport, you'll learn tips, techniques, and ideas for remembering your experiences in style.

IN THIS CHAPTER:

- Creating an album to document a memorable vacation

- Finding fun and exciting ways to record your travels and include your memorabilia

- Creating unique traditional scrapbook pages celebrating your vacations

Professional
B E A C H   F A M I L Y

This year, we had all the gear. We had the cabana, the umbrella, the sand chairs, the toys, the little table and the snacks. The boys are always delighted by the beach. There is nothing better than feeling like you are playing in a giant sand box. Mommy and Lily were the only ones who napped in the cabana, but the rest of our gear had a workout as the boys kept busy finding treasures, chasing birds and playing in the surf.

J E K Y L L   I S L A N D
Summer 2004

Chapter **4**

Road Trip: The Vacation Album

Whether it's a day trip to the zoo or a week in the Caribbean, everyone needs a break now and then. Vacations refresh us and allow us time for renewal and reflection. They also offer the chance to spend extended amounts of time with family and friends. Creating a special album for a memorable vacation is an ideal way to preserve your memories from your best vacations.

Mt. McKinley

RECORDING YOUR TRIP

If you're like many people, vacations are probably some of the most-photographed events in your life. Even people who aren't typically camera savvy love to photograph the memories created during their vacations. Filling a special album with all those photos is the perfect way to create a lasting memento to celebrate your vacation.

GETTING STARTED

Preparing to create your vacation album is easy. Simply gather your photographs from the vacation you want to scrap. Take a moment to group together similar photos according to event. Select at least two 4×6-inch photos from each event to include in your album. Then write a quick caption for each set of photos or event. You can jot these down on the album planning worksheet included in Appendix B.

CREATING THE ALBUM

To begin your album, gather the following supplies:

- **8×8-inch Scrapbook Album with Picture Window (KI Memories)**
- **12×12-inch Patterned Paper and cardstock— "Deep Sea" collection (KI Memories)**
- **Black metal photo corners (Daisy D's)**
- **"Studio" alphabet die set and hand tool (QuickKutz)**
- **Black cardstock**
- **White acrylic paint and foam brush**
- *Mini Minerals* **(Outrageous Daisy)**
- **Computer for journaling**
- **Paper trimmer, adhesive**

These fun photographs matched up great with the journaling text describing the glacier boat tour.

After you've gathered your photographs and captions, you're ready to begin making your special scrapbook.

This fun album coordinates perfectly with the patterned papers for this project and was the best choice for creating this album featuring a trip to Alaska.

Begin by cutting a sheet of patterned paper to 8×8 inches. This forms the base for your title page. Select a favorite photo from your vacation, and attach it to the bottom half of the page. Attach a metal photo corner to each corner of the photograph.

Next, use a dry foam brush to swipe acrylic paint across the top half of the page. Let this dry. Use the QuickKutz system to die cut the letters for your chosen title from black cardstock. Adhere the letters to the page.

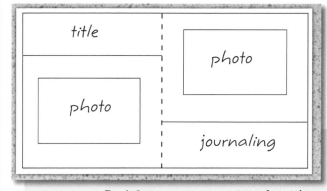

Each 2-page spread consists of a title, 2 photographs, and a journaling strip.

Your completed title page should look something like this.

When you've created your title page, it's a good idea to take a moment to prepare your journaling for the album. Refer to your album planning worksheet for the journaling you've already written. Using your computer, print this text onto a sheet of patterned cardstock. (See Chapter 3 if you need help printing on 12×12 paper). Cut the journaling for each 2-page spread into an 8×1½-inch block.

Now it's time to create the interior pages of your album. This is a quick and easy process that involves only some simple measuring and cutting. The basic interior layout is the same for each 2-page spread.

To begin making your first spread, follow these simple steps:

1. Select one sheet of patterned paper to cut a block of paper for your title. (Often, the pattern you used for your title page makes an excellent choice for your page titles as well.) Cut a block of the paper measuring 8×2½ inches.

2. Select a coordinating pattern, and cut two blocks, one measuring 8×5½ inches and a second measuring 8×6½ inches.

3. Using the 8×8-inch sheets that came inside your album as a guide, piece the pieces together to create two 8×8-inch pages, adding an 8×1½-inch journaling block at the bottom of the second page. If you want, you can add a small strip of a contrasting pattern to the bottom of your journaling block for added interest.

4. Following the layout sketch, add your photographs to the pages.

5. Create your page title by again dry brushing white acrylic paint across the paper, letting it dry, and then adhering your die cut title on top.

6. Finally, use the Mini Minerals to create photo corners for your photographs. Attach the rocks in small clusters using a strong, acid-free adhesive.

Creating photo corners with Mini Minerals is quite simple and produces a truly unique look in your album.

This spread coordinates perfectly and provides a simple and classic showcase for these photographs, as well as the memory that accompanies them.

7. **Simply repeat steps 1 through 6 for the remaining photographs and memories you'd like to include in your album.**

FINAL TOUCHES

After you've completed your album page spreads, you might find yourself with remaining photographs or memories that didn't yet make it into your album. Perhaps you had a single photograph of a special event, photographs in a size or orientation different from your others, or memories you'd like to include that don't have photographs to match. Creating an additional page or two to hold these items is a piece of cake. Try one of the following options to customize your album according to whatever specific needs you might have:

- **Place two vertically oriented photos side by side on a single page of your layout. Because 4×6-inch photos at full size will be a tight fit, consider reducing them in size or cropping out background elements for a clean look.**

- **Create a single large journaling block detailing your favorite moments from your vacation, even if you don't have specific photos to accompany them.**

- **Create a photo collage containing numerous extra photographs or small details.**

- **Add a 2-page spread for your memorabilia. Include postcards, ticket stubs, and more. (See Chapter 3 for more information on preserving your memorabilia and making sure it's safe for your scrapbooks.)**

Place these pages either at the front or back of your album, whatever seems to create the best fit for your personal project.

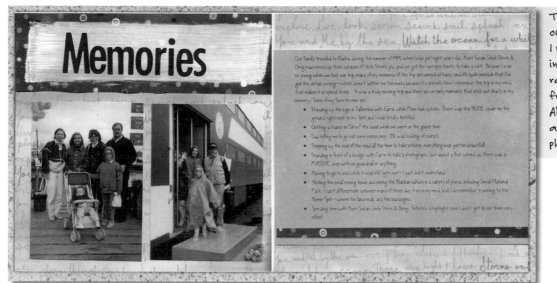

This page worked out fantastically. I was able to include some random memories from my trip to Alaska as well as a pair of vertical photos.

The last step to creating your perfect album is to select a favorite photo for the picture window on the cover of the album itself. A 5×5-inch print fits quite nicely.

Whether you're scrapbooking a day trip to the zoo or a month-long European excursion, this simple vacation album can be the perfect match for your vacation photos and memories. It's simple enough to create in a weekend and beautiful enough to cherish for a lifetime.

REMEMBERING YOUR VACATIONS

Don't have the time to create an entire album celebrating one vacation? Or perhaps you only have a handful of photos from a past trip and don't feel they'd fill an entire album. Making traditional scrapbook pages to feature your vacation photos is a fun way to include them in your albums without a lot of time or expense.

In Chapter 1, we learned that "traditional" scrapbooking consists of creating an album of same-sized layouts (generally 12×12-inches or 8½×11-inches), and placing them in a single album in chronological order, regardless of theme or design. This system still works well for many individuals. Most scrapbook artists keep one or two of these albums on hand, even when devoting the majority of their energy to more theme-based projects.

Creating vacation layouts for your standard-sized albums is a fun and effective way to scrapbook your vacation memories—particularly when you're short on photographs, time, or energy.

Try one of the following ideas for your first vacation layout. (If you get stuck trying to design your page, refer to Chapter 3 for some helpful design tips.)

- **Include a group of photos on a single page that reflect the mood of your trip. Try a collage of photos or a simple blocked design.**

- Create a page (or set of pages) featuring your to-the-minute vacation itinerary—what you did and when you did it.

- Stuck without photos? Find a set of postcards from your vacation location, add some journaling, and you're all set. If you didn't happen to pick up any postcards while on vacation, try searching online for area retailers, or visit eBay.com to see what kinds of postcard collections are currently offered for sale.

- Feature a "top 10" list on your scrapbook page, celebrating your 10 favorite moments from your trip.

This layout uses only two supplies—cardstock and a computer font. Despite its simplicity, this layout beautifully shows the fun and feeling of the family's beach excursion.

(Layout by Julie Ann Stella)

SCRAPBOOKING SCENERY AND LANDMARKS

We all take those photos—shot after shot of the beautiful mountains, the endless ocean, or the Statue of Liberty. After our vacation is complete, we often end up with an entire roll (or sometimes more) of film featuring nothing but these photographs. But what do you *do* with them? There is indeed a place for these photographs in your scrapbooks!

Try one of these fun ideas for including these photos in your albums:

- Select one favorite photo and enlarge it to 5×7 or even 8×10, and use it as the focal point of your layout. Reduce your others to wallet size or smaller and use them to frame your focal point photo.

This fantastic layout features only one photograph, yet it fully captures the emotion and mood of the artist's trip to a spa in Lake Austin, Texas.

(Layout by Monica Schoenemann)

- Spend some time journaling about how you felt when you were looking at the subject of your photograph and what prompted you to take the photograph. Pair this with a single photograph to create a beautiful and emotionally charged scrapbook page.

- Create a layout featuring a collage of several of your scenic photos.

- Enlarge your favorite vacation photo and print it on iron-on transfer paper or printable fabric. Then, add it to the cover of your vacation album.

- Turn your favorite photos into magnets for your refrigerator. (See Chapter 19 for instructions.)

A great way to feature landmarks on your scrapbook pages is to use your landmark photo as the focal point of your layout and then add smaller, complementing photographs to showcase your entire experience, as seen in this great layout.

(Layout by Debbie Hodge)

This layout focuses on the beautiful photographs it features. The enlarged photographs help keep the emphasis on the photographs themselves, which is perfect. The photo on the left flips up to reveal the artist's journaling about the trip.

(Layout by April Derrick)

HIGHLY ACTIVE VACATIONS

For many people, vacations are centered around activities such as snowboarding, skiing, kayaking, rowing, and even cliff diving! We explore scrap-booking sports in greater detail later on (see Chapter 8), so for now, let's take a minute to discuss vacation-specific sporting memories.

These types of memories can often pose a challenge to the scrapbook artist because of the lack of high-quality photos that result. If you're skydiving, chances are you're not snapping your camera at the same time! (Although hopefully someone on the ground can snap a photograph for you.) Despite the less-than-stellar photographs that often result from these types of activities (or the absence of photos entirely), your vacation sports memories are still most definitely scrapbook-worthy.

Try one of these quick fixes for including active memories in your albums:

- Enlarge a single photograph you do have and pair it with journaling about your experience.

- Find a *stock photo* online of the equipment needed for your adventure, and use it on a layout in place of your own photographs.

SCRAP SPEAK

A **stock photo** is an image that can be used in your album in place of photos you have taken yourself. Stock photos can be found online, often for free or at a low cost, and are often

royalty-free, making them a safe and legal choice for your scrapbook album. (Be sure to check each site's license agreement for information on how their stock photos can be legally used.) My favorite site for these types of photographs is www.istockphoto.com.

SCRAPBOOKING YOUR DAY TRIPS

Travel layouts don't always have to be about week-long vacations and trips to exotic places. Traveling is something most of us do every day, so don't forget to let those memories shine in your scrapbooks as well. Try scrapbooking some of these fun everyday moments:

- **Day trips to the zoo, an amusement part, or other local attraction.**

- **A visit to a museum. (Be sure to check with museum authorities, as many places have rules against flash photography.)**

- **Time spent traveling to a relative's home or even a work-related conference or event.**

- **A visit to a large city near your home.**

- **The places you visit every week—yes, even your grocery store layout will be interesting a few years down the road!**

- **Your favorite local hangouts: the places to which you return time after time. Pair these photos with journaling about why you're so in love with that location!**

Kayaking was more fun than I though it would be. I sat in front and Kevin in back. It took us a little while to get in sync with each other, but after we did we led the pack. Our guide took us around a cove to where the locals lived. We were able to see how they lived, which was much different from what we were use to. Some of the local boys swam out to our kayak and tried to sell us shells. Overall, it was a good excursion.

Kayaking

This artist was lucky enough to get a trio of fun photos from her kayaking experience. She matched them up with some insightful journaling about her experience, and the result is this well-designed page.

(Layout by Amy Alvis)

Capture your photos from a water park visit on a fun layout
like this one, featuring products from Karen Foster Design.

(Layout by Kris Ortale, owner, Memories on Fifth)

This pretty layout showcases the artist's daughter
playing at Dow Gardens—one of their family's
favorite places to travel.

(Layout by Kay Rogers)

GIRL, YOU ARE **ADDICTED** TO
WATER. EVERY TIME WE GO TO
DOW GARDENS YOU PLAY IN THE
WATER FEATURE. AND THE LOOK
OF SHEER **GLEE** IN YOUR EYES THE
FIRST TIME THE WATER SPLASHES
YOU IS A SIGHT TO BEHOLD. IT
DOESN'T BOTHER YOU ONE BIT
THAT WE HAVE TO CLIMB BACK IN
THE CAR WITH YOU SOAKING WET.
SO I DON'T LET IT BOTHER ME.
KEEP HAVING **FUN**, MY GIRL!

THE LEAST YOU NEED TO KNOW

- Creating a special album to commemorate your favorite vacation is
  fun and easy.

- Adapting the album design to meet
  your own needs is simple and results
  in a truly personal creation.

- There are many ways to include your
  vacation memories in your traditional
  scrapbooks without spending a lot of
  money or time on your pages.

- All travel memories—no matter how
  seemingly insignificant they might
  be—are worthy of scrapbooking and
  should be included in your albums.

IN THIS CHAPTER:

- Creating an album celebrating the holiday traditions from your childhood as well as your adult years

- Using the Bay Box Album system from Scrapworks to create the easiest album you'll ever make

- Traditional scrapbook ideas for annual holiday celebrations and birthdays

BIRTHDAY BALLOONS

Nicole's Sweet 16

er about the candy. And since I've always
carve pumpkins either. Halloween was still
en I was little, though it seemed like I ofter
before. During a few years in middle sch
nd Stephanie's basement, along with our
o recall a favorite costume, but I do remem
heerleader.

My siblings and I each got to
cary, but all of them had unique
course, there were costumes. The
over up the costumes with our
ne, my favorite Halloween costume

198

Chapter **5**

Happy Holidays: Celebrating Your Annual Traditions

My mother once told me that she found an undeveloped roll of film in her desk. After taking it to be processed, she discovered an entire year of holidays on that single roll of film. Even for people who aren't wild about using their cameras, holidays are often a highly photographed time. Creating a scrapbook to showcase your holiday memories is the perfect way to get your holiday photos out of the dusty boxes and into a beautiful album.

CREATING YOUR SCRAPBOOK

What do you do with those mountains of holiday photographs? (Especially when you have more than 20 years' worth of photos, and you only really like a handful of them?) This album is the ideal solution. Using a *Bay Box Album,* you'll create a fantastic keepsake you'll treasure—and add to—for years to come.

SCRAP SPEAK

A **Bay Box Album** is a specialty scrapbook album produced by Scrapworks. Featuring 3 styles of divided page protectors designed for 4×6-inch photographs, this album system is ideal for individuals who want to create a scrapbook but have limited time or resources to devote to page design.

GETTING STARTED

To prepare for your album's creation, all you need to do is gather a few photographs from each holiday you celebrate throughout the calendar year. You might want to include birthdays as well. Selecting photos from your own childhood, as well as your spouse's childhood, can be particularly fun.

An album planning worksheet in Appendix B can assist you with your photo and holiday selection. Consider the following holidays:

- **New Year's Day**
- **Valentine's Day**
- **St. Patrick's Day**
- **Independence Day**
- **Easter**
- **Passover**
- **Halloween**
- **Thanksgiving**
- **Chanukah**
- **Christmas**
- **Kwanzaa**

Your family might celebrate different holidays according to your religious or cultural preferences. Be sure to select a group of holidays that best works for your family's needs.

Gather two to eight photographs for each holiday, and be sure to note the year in which each was taken. When you have your photographs, it's time to begin creating your project.

MAKING YOUR SCRAPBOOK

Begin by gathering the materials you'll need to create your album:

- **8×12-inch fabric-covered Bay Box Album (Scrapworks)**
- **12×12-inch Patterned Paper ("Shades of" collection by Karen Foster Design)**
- **White textured cardstock (Bazzill Basics)**
- **Rub-on letters in various colors (Scrapworks)**
- **Holiday Die Cuts (QuicKutz)**
- **Computer for journaling**
- **Paper trimmer, adhesive**

This gorgeous album provides the showcase for your holiday photo collection.

Creating the pages for your holiday album is a simple process. Because the page protectors included in your album are already divided into sections, there's no sketch to follow or design work to do. Simply add the photographs and journaling blocks into the presized sections, and your page is nearly complete.

Because the page protectors included in Bay Box Albums come in a few different layout designs, it's a good idea to work on this scrapbook in order, front to back. This saves you time later on and ensures that you work with the correct design for each holiday. If you want all your page layouts to match exactly, simply purchase a refill pack in your favorite style.

Let's begin by creating a title page. I used the full-size 8×12-inch page design (Style A) to create my title page. Follow these easy steps to create your own:

1. Cut a multicolor sheet of patterned paper to 8×12 inches.

2. Add your title to the upper left corner of your page using white rub-on letters.

3. Mat a favorite family photograph on white textured cardstock. Add to the layout in the center of your paper.

4. If you want, print a subtitle on a scrap of white textured cardstock. Simply adhere a scrap of paper to a standard sheet of printer paper using removable adhesive, print, and remove the scrap from the paper. Adhere this to the bottom of your layout.

That's all there is to it!

After you've completed your title page, add it to your album. Turn the page, and begin work on the layout for your first holiday.

This title page contains all the elements necessary for the perfect introduction to your album.

Creating layouts for each holiday you plan to include is a simple process:

1. Begin by selecting the page layout you plan to use. You can complete a single page for each holiday, or create a 2-page spread. Remember that each style of page protector can be combined with others to create several different layout styles.

2. Decide where you'd like to place your photographs. Be sure to leave at least two spots open.

3. Using your alphabet rub-ons, add the year in which each photo was taken to a corner of the photograph.

4. Add your photos to the page protectors.

5. Cut out two blocks from patterned paper in a coordinating color, one each to fit your empty sections.

6. Add two question marks to one of the empty blocks, and add it to your layout. This is so you can add a special photo to your album in the future.

Finally, you'll want to create the journaling block for your page. All it takes is three easy steps:

1. **Using rub-on letters, add the name of the holiday you're commemorating in a coordinating color.**

2. **Using your computer, print your journaling on white textured cardstock. A good idea is to reflect on each holiday, write about what it means to you, and share a favorite memory or two.**

3. **Finally, use the QuicKutz hand tool and holiday dies to create a themed accent for your page. (See Chapter 3 if you need assistance with die cutting.)**

PICTURE THIS

For a unique touch, consider having each member of your family contribute to the journaling on each page. You'll create a truly personal feeling for your album.

This page design uses two of the standard 4x6-inch page protectors (Style C). The fun photographs and colors create a truly great look.

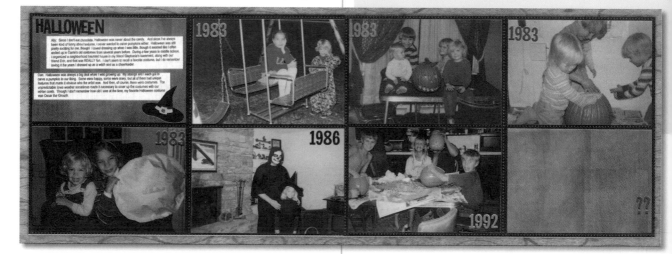

When working with Style B page protectors, simply mat larger photos on textured cardstock to fill each partition of the layout design. This is a great way to include vertically oriented photographs.

ROOM TO GROW

After you've created page layouts for each holiday you want to include, you're almost done. Because the Bay Box Album features a picture window on the front cover, it's a great idea to include your album's title in that space.

To create a title for your album, simply cut a small piece of patterned paper and add your title using rub-on letters. Place it in the window on your album cover, and your album is complete.

The beauty of your completed holiday album is that it isn't actually complete—and might never be! By leaving a blank space on each holiday's

PICTURE THIS

Instead of including the title on your album's cover, select a favorite holiday photo for a personal touch.

layout, you've created room to add photographs from holiday celebrations yet to come. Try changing this photo year after year, or simply wait a few years and add a special one later on. Remember, you can always add page protectors to your album and accommodate many more years of holiday memories.

HOLIDAY CELEBRATIONS

Now that you've completed your very first holiday album, you're probably in the mood to scrapbook even more. Holidays are some of the most fun events to include in your scrapbooks—probably because they bring back so many happy memories.

Maybe you'd like to create a special layout featuring just last year's Halloween photos. Or perhaps you feel the need to tell a special holiday story from this year's Chanukah celebration. No matter what your personal need, there are numerous ways to include holiday pages in your traditional scrapbook albums.

MEMORABLE HOLIDAY MOMENTS

Each year brings many new memories to the table, and despite the fact that many things about holiday celebrations remain the same from year to year, there's always a new story to tell. Try scrapbooking your most recent holiday moments in one of the following ways:

- **Create a 2-page spread featuring all the photos from this year's celebration.**

- **Enlarge a favorite photograph and use it as the focal point for your layout, and accompany it with the story behind the photo.**

- **Create a list of your favorite moments from your holiday celebration. Include favorite gifts (both given and received), funny stories and quotes, and embarrassing moments.**

- **Create a layout using a large pocket to hold all the greeting cards you received.**

- **Make a scrapbook page from your child's perspective on the holiday being featured on your layout.**

This layout does a fantastic job of featuring a lot of photos in a small amount of space. Try a similar approach when working with a large number of holiday photographs.

(Layout by Angie Hagist)

Showcasing your child's Halloween costume on a scrapbook page is a must every year. This adorable layout does it perfectly.

(Layout by Sheredian Vickers, Scrapjazz.com design team member)

This Valentine's Day layout is simply precious and does a fantastic job portraying this child's excitement about the big day.

(Layout by Monica Schoenemann)

TRADITIONS AND FOOD

Certain aspects of each holiday make us anticipate it eagerly, year after year. For many of us, it's the traditions and food surrounding each holiday that cause our excitement to grow. When the season finally arrives, participating in these traditions brings us closer to our families and friends and enables us to experience a feeling of warmth and familiarity.

From traditional meals to bizarre family pastimes (my family plays a wild game of Bingo every year after Thanksgiving dinner), all these items deserve a special place in your scrapbook albums.

Try creating a scrapbook page featuring your favorite tradition or food item, or one celebrating a new spin you've put on an old favorite.

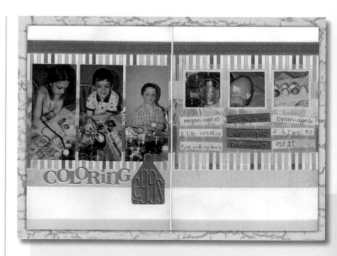

These children really enjoy coloring eggs for Easter each year. Try creating a page showcasing your own children's springtime creations.

(Layout by Rachael Giallongo)

This mother was worried that her young child might get too caught up in the massive amount of Halloween candy offered each year, so she provided her son with a healthier alternative, which he appeared to enjoy even more, creating a new tradition for this family.

(Layout by Linda Harrison)

If you celebrate Christmas, it's always a great idea to have a quick photo shoot in front of the tree. This layout complements the beauty and lighting of the tree just beautifully.

(Layout by Andrea Steed, co-founder Scrapjazz.com)

Lighting the Menorah is an emotionally and religiously significant time for Jewish families. This layout perfectly captures the occasion, keeping the focus on the photos and the moment at hand.

(Layout by Kathi Rerek)

CELEBRATING BIRTHDAYS

Birthdays are a time like no other holiday. For an entire day, the world celebrates you. Who could ask for anything more? Many of the album projects in this book make wonderful birthday gifts for others. To scrapbook photos from the event itself, consider one of these great ideas:

- Create a page celebrating how the birthday boy or girl has changed over the past year.

- Highlight the day's itinerary on a special layout.

- Include a list of the gifts and cards received on a scrapbook page.

- For surprise birthday parties, use a hidden or moving element to convey the excitement of the party.

- Feature a list of the birthday boy or girl's favorite things at that age on a layout along with photographs from the child's party.

- Record your child's birthday wishes on a scrapbook page. Add photos of the birthday boy or girl blowing out the candles on the cake for a perfect match.

- All grown up and not having a party? Consider simply taking a photograph of yourself on your birthday and matching it with some introspective journaling about your life. (See Chapter 12 for tons of great ideas.)

A young girl's birthday dreams take center stage on this pretty scrapbook page.

(Layout by Kay Rogers)

This simple and well-designed layout enables these fun photographs to take center stage. Notice the unique journaling added to the photo itself.

(Layout by Rachael Giallongo)

THE LEAST YOU NEED TO KNOW

- Use the Bay Box Album system by Scrapworks to create a unique and lasting holiday memory album.

- Adding to your album year after year is easy and fun.

- It's easy to create meaningful holiday scrapbook pages showcasing your current memories as well as your unique family traditions.

- Birthdays are important events to include in your scrapbooks. Try creating a unique birthday layout to include in your traditional scrapbook albums.

IN THIS CHAPTER:

- Commemorating your baby's first year with an ABC album
- Getting started: a sample ABC list
- Journaling and page ideas for celebrating your child
- Capturing your emotions in your scrapbook

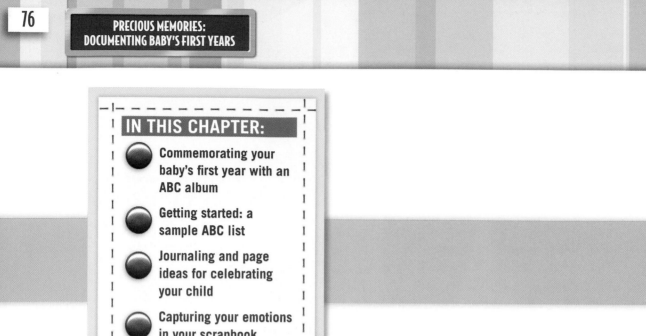

pickle

WONDER

Chapter 6

Precious Memories: Documenting Baby's First Years

The addition of a new baby to a family causes all sorts of changes and excitement. Babies bring hope, joy, and loads of new experiences. Scrapbooking the life of your baby can be quite daunting at first.

Creating a small album themed around your child's first year proves to be the perfect solution. You can enjoy your child's greatest moments and compile them into this easy project—an ABC album you can complete in a weekend.

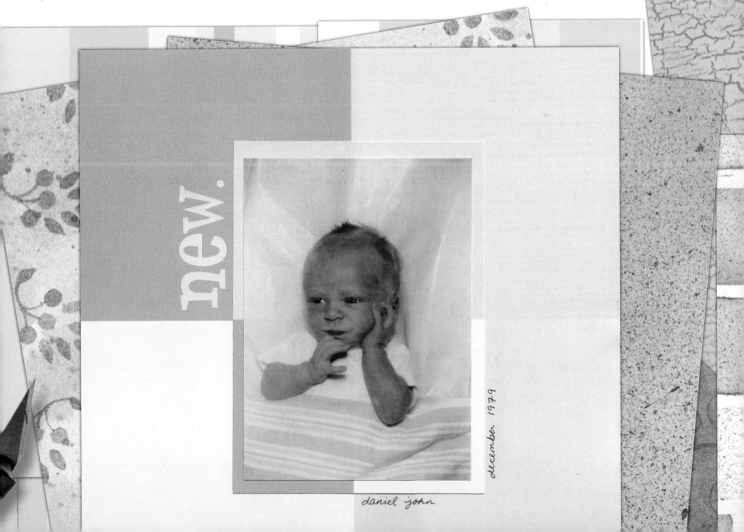

new.

december 1979

daniel john

THE PERFECT ALBUM

Your child's first year has come and gone far more quickly than you anticipated it would. If you're like many people, you're now facing an incredible pile of photos. You're not quite sure how you ended up with so many, and not one of them has found its way into a scrapbook or photo album. An ABC album is the perfect solution.

SCRAP SPEAK

An **ABC album** contains one page for each letter of the alphabet, usually related to one specific theme or event.

The first year in any child's life is full of special memories, first experiences, holidays, and many special events. Putting them into an ABC album is the perfect way to represent all these moments without feeling the need to scrapbook every single photo from your pile.

GETTING STARTED

The first step in creating an ABC album is to select your photographs and individual page titles. The layout of this book requires that you choose one word or phrase for each letter of the alphabet, along with one or two matching photographs. (Turn to Appendix B for an album-planning worksheet that will assist you through this selection process.)

Because your page titles are the heart of the project, you'll want to be sure you've selected them before you do anything else. Select one word for each letter representing an event or moment in your child's life. Here are some ideas to get you started:

A	Adorable, Angel, Amazing, Aunt
B	Blankie, Bottle, Bath, Birthday, Baptism
C	Cute, Cuddles, Crying, Cousins, Christmas, Chanukah
D	Daddy, Diaper, Discover, Dream
E	Eat, Easter, Energetic, Entertainment
F	Family, First, Fabulous, Fingers
G	Generations, Giggle, Grow, Grandparents, Gifts
H	Halloween, Happy, Hugs, Hospital, Haircut
I	Ice Cream, Interesting, Immunizations
J	Jammies, Juice, Joy, Jump
K	Kisses, Kind, Kwanzaa, Kids
L	Love, Lullaby, Little
M	Mommy, Mine, Music, Milk
N	Namesake, New, Nursery, Naptime
O	One, Onesie, Open
P	Play, Peek-a-Boo, Parents, Party
Q	Quiet, Quick, Quilt
R	Reading, Rattle, Roll Over
S	Singing, Sisters, Story Time, Swing, Standing
T	Toys, Teeth, Toes, Teddy, Thanksgiving
U	Uncle, Unhappy, University (Future Graduate)
V	Visiting, Video, Vegetables
W	Wonder, Waving, Water, Wiggle, Walk
X	eXcitement, X-mas, eXtraordinary
Y	Yawn, Yummy, Yard
Z	ZZZs, Zoo, Zany

If you get stuck, try using a fun sentence or phrase instead of a single word. You'll find that this gives you a few more options when working with difficult letters.

Very Special

Use your letter to begin a phrase that describes your subject, such as Very Special.

This fun yet pretty album is an ideal choice for your ABC scrapbook.

PICTURE THIS

Don't forget to consider using proper names in your album. Consider special people, places, and pets.

After you've selected your page titles, be sure you have at least one 4×6-inch photograph to accompany each word. You'll also want to select two additional photos: one for your album cover and a second for the title page.

SELECTING YOUR MATERIALS

To create this project, you'll need the following:

- 8½×8½-inch Post-bound Album with a photo window (Studio K by K&Company)

- White satin ribbon, ⅜ inches wide (Offray)

- Assorted patterned papers, alphabets, accents, and embellishments in a variety of themes, styles, and colors

- Paper trimmer, scissors, black pen, adhesive, computer for journaling (optional)

PAPER CUTS

When you're purchasing an album, be sure you double-check the number of page protectors included. The album shown here comes with 20 protectors, but many albums come with only 10 page protectors, so you might need to purchase a package of refill protectors when you buy your album. You'll need 14 for this project.

As you've learned, usually when designing a theme album, it's wise to select papers and embellishments created by the same manufacturer or designed in the same style to ensure a perfect match. This album is an exception, however. Because the lives of babies are so varied and exciting, it only follows that your scrapbook should have a varied and exciting look, too. Choose your papers and embellishments to match the theme and mood of each page. Don't spend too much time worrying about matching all the pages.

This Halloween-themed paper and sticker set from Karen Foster Design is the perfect match for these fun holiday photos.

CREATING THE PAGES

Now that you have your page titles, photographs, and products selected, the fun can truly begin! You can work in any order, but I recommend starting at the beginning of the alphabet and working straight through to the end. It's a fun way to see your album begin to take shape, and you'll be less likely to make mistakes.

The basic page design for an ABC album is fairly simple. Each page consists of the featured letter in the upper left or right corner, with the title running across the bottom of the page. One or two photos per page is ideal.

Letter placement can be tricky, so take extra time deciding on word placement when planning your pages. When the album lies open, you want the pages on the left to have their letter in the left corner; likewise for right-side pages. Think of each two pages as a spread, and you'll stay clear of trouble. Working through the alphabet in order and placing your pages into the album as you go assures that your album stays on track.

Follow these simple steps to create your first page:

1. **Start with a full sheet of patterned paper. If the paper you chose is larger than 8½×8½ inches, cut it to size using a paper trimmer.**

2. **Adhere your photo(s) to the center of the page, adding a photo mat from another patterned paper or cardstock if you like.**

3. **Add your title to the bottom of the page.**

4. **Place your "A" in the top-left corner of the page.**

5. **If you want, you can add embellishments and accents, but it's not necessary. The photos are the highlight of this album. Adding too many extras detracts from your photos and the simplicity of your album.**

The basic layout design for ABC album pages.

A	B
photo	photo / photo
adorable	blankie

A perfect first page.

Now you want to add your completed page to your album. Open your album, and turn the first page so you're looking at the page protectors that hold your first 2-page spread. Insert your "A" page into the page protector on the left.

You're now ready to begin your second page. Follow the same steps you used to create your first page, but instead of placing your letter in the top-left corner, place it in the top-right corner. When you're finished, slide your "B" page into the album next to your "A" page.

After you've gotten the hang of it, the album will come together fairly quickly. Simply repeat these basic steps to create pages for all 26 letters of the alphabet. Be sure to make each page unique to reflect the mood of each particular idea. Although you don't need to worry about matching each page to the others, do take a moment to notice what pages lay next to each other. Using complementary colors or a similar product can create a visually pleasing effect.

The use of grosgrain ribbon on both pages ties them together and makes the entire spread more pleasing to the eye.

FINAL STEPS

The ABC pages of your album are fun and exciting, and they convey the most important moments of your child's first year. You've created 26 pages, and your album is almost complete. A title page, closing page, and decorated cover brings it all together.

Start by creating your title page. On this page, you introduce the concept of the album as well as identify the subject and timeframe of the album's contents. A typical introduction page should include the following information:

- **The album's title. ("Now I Know My ABCs" and "A is for …" are good choices.)**

- **The subject's name.**

- **The timeframe in which the photos were taken. (Typically, this is the baby's date of birth through his or her first birthday.)**

Again, cut your paper to 8½×8½ inches if necessary. Add the necessary information using your computer, a journaling pen, or alphabet of your choice. Finally, add a photo of your subject. Slide the completed page into the first page protector in your album.

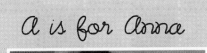

A is for Anna

An alphabetical celebration of your first year

January 17, 2004 - January 17, 2005

This fun title page uses computer printed journaling for a playful and professional look.

The last page in your album is one of the most important pages. First and foremost, be sure you include your own name on this page. Future generations will enjoy seeing the photos from your child's first year, but they'll also want to know the identity of the album's creator. Beyond that, it's up to you. You can conclude your album in a number of fun and interesting ways. Consider the following:

- **A "top 10" list of funny or special memories from the year.**

- **A list of reasons why you love your child.**

- **A letter to your child, signed in your own handwriting.**

- **A small piece of memorabilia, such as a lock of hair, enclosed in a pocket on the page. (See Chapter 3 for more information on including memorabilia in your scrapbooks.)**

When you've completed your closing page, slide it into the last spot in your album. If any empty page protectors remain, remove them.

Open your album cover and tie a length of ribbon around the left side, about halfway between the spine and the photo window. Finish with a simple bow for a fun and elegant look. Finally, close the album and add a final photo to the window on the album cover.

Your final result is a wonderful keepsake album your child will cherish for years to come.

PICTURE THIS

ABC albums aren't just for babies. Try creating them for weddings, gifts for special friends, and more. Visit www.creativescrapbooking.com/abclists.htm for ABC lists to help you get started on a number of topics.

This personal letter creates an emotional and significant ending to the album.

CELEBRATING BABY

Notice how the tags on this layout create the perfect title. Another tag pulls out from behind the photo to reveal additional journaling.

(Layout by Sheredian Vickers, Scrapjazz. com design team; photo by The Studio in Target)

Perhaps you want to celebrate a special baby in your life but don't want to create an entire album. Maybe your friend or sibling has recently given birth, or perhaps you're looking for a way to scrap just a few special photos. You can include babies in your traditional albums in many different ways.

Consider taking the ABC album concept and adapting it to a single page. In this fantastic layout, each letter of the child's first name is matched with a personality trait beginning with the same letter. The end result is priceless.

CONSIDER THE FACTS

Consider creating a scrapbook featuring the statistics and stories about your child and how he or she came to be. From documenting your pregnancy to your child's first hospital visitors, you can include these memories and facts in your scrapbook in a number of fun ways. Try creating pages about the following:

- **Your child's birth weight and length**

- **Your baby's first gift**

- **The meaning of your child's name and how you selected it**

- **The events of your baby's time in the hospital**

- **Your child's zodiac sign or your child's Chinese New Year sign**

- **Major events and statistics from your child's year of birth (These details will be fun to read about for years to come.)**

Scrapbooking about your child's zodiac sign is a fun and interesting way to describe his or her personality.

(Layout by Teresa Olier)

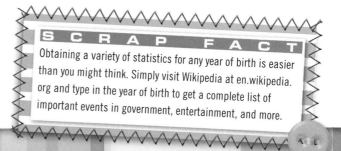

This layout captures the significance of the child's birth as well as the events of the year in which it occurred.

(Layout by Andrea Steed, co-founder, Scrapjazz.com)

This gorgeous layout captures the story behind the child's name beautifully.

(Layout by Heidi M. Deck

FABULOUS FIRSTS

In the life of a baby, there are many "firsts." From the first tears to the first steps (and all the moments in between), many milestones can be celebrated. Consider scrapbooking about your child's very own firsts:

- **Rolling over and sitting up**
- **Crawling and walking**
- **Haircut**
- **Ride in a car**
- **Tooth**
- **Smile**

This layout perfectly captures the excitement of bath time.

(Layout by Linda Harrison)

This layout captures the joy of this child's first time in a swimming pool.

Even the youngest people have friends. Be sure to capture those special first friendships.

(Layout by Alecia Ackerman Grimm)

EVERYDAY MOMENTS

For infants, day-to-day life is anything but routine, as babies are constantly learning about and exploring the world around them. Don't forget to capture these special moments in your albums. The following ideas are just a few great ways to get started:

- **Naptime**
- **Taking baths**
- **Daycare routines and schedules**
- **Bottles, feeding, and favorite foods**
- **Friendships**
- **Talking a walk outside in the stroller**
- **Relaxing in the baby swing**

EMOTIONAL MESSAGES

Babies have their own unique way of filling everyone around them with love. They naturally make us smile and give us hope for the future. We also feel scared for them, bewildered by them, and even sometimes get a little angry with them. Capture the emotional moments of parenthood, grandparenthood, or any other unique relationship you share with a special little someone on a scrapbook page. Your 3-month-old infant might not yet understand what exactly you mean when you say "I love you." But as your child grows older, he or she will truly appreciate the fact that you chose to record your thoughts and feelings on paper.

Try creating a page about your hopes and dreams for your child, as well as the questions you have. What will your child be when he grows up? What kind of person will she marry? These excellent questions would provide a great foundation for a scrapbook page.

This layout reflects on the child's future as
seen through the eyes of his grandmother.

(Layout by Sheredian Vickers,
Scrapjazz.com design team)

Sometimes there are things you want a child to
know, even when they are too young to understand
them. Consider capturing your thoughts on a
scrapbook page for the child to read in the future.

A letter from aunt to niece provides a
touching foundation for this scrapbook page.

THE LEAST YOU NEED TO KNOW

 An ABC album is a simple and
effective way to preserve a lot of
memories from baby's first year.

Avoid mistakes when creating an
ABC album simply by working in
order and placing completed pages
into your album as you create them.

Consider creating a scrapbook page
about the major events in the life of
your infant.

Recording your emotions on a
scrapbook page can be a powerful
way to bond with your infant, even
if he or she won't be able to read or
understand the message until years
later.

IN THIS CHAPTER:

- Creating a scrapbook album to celebrate school-year events

- Fun ways to commemorate accomplishments, lessons learned, and more

- Scrapbook page ideas for back to school, dances, field trips, and more

- Celebrating graduations

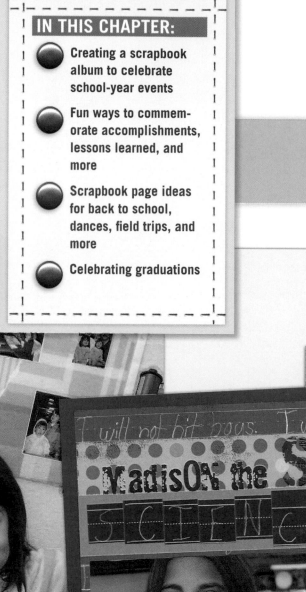

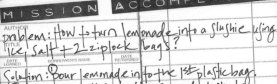

Madison the SIXTH GRADE SCIENCE EXPERT A+

I will not hit boys. I will not hit boys. I will not hit

MISSION ACCOMPLISHED

AUTHOR / TITLE: problem: How to turn lemonade into a slushie using Ice, salt + 2 ziplock bags?

DATE LOANED / BORROWER'S NAME / DATE RETURNED

Solution: Pour lemonade into the 1st plastic bag. ② put ice + salt into the second plastic bag. ③ insert bag 1 into bag 2. ④ Knead the two bags until frozen. ⑤ Remove swshie, pour into cup + Enjoy!

this stuff tastes awesome, but it's freezing cold!

Chapter **7**

School Days: Scrapbooking the Educational Experience

Going to school is the one thing virtually all people in the world have in common. At some point, in some way, we all go to school and are given the education we need to succeed in the world. Everyone's educational experiences are different, but they are all worth celebrating.

Consider creating a scrapbook to capture a memorable year in the education of your child. Whether you're scrapbooking preschool events, high school moments, or homeschool adventures, this super-colorful (and super-simple!) album is the answer you're looking for.

CELEBRATING THE FORMATIVE YEARS

One of the biggest hurdles in scrapbooking school-related events can be obtaining and sorting the photographs. If your child goes to school all day while you're at work, how are you supposed to take photographs? There are a number of solutions to this problem, so don't start panicking yet!

- **Attend parent-teacher events, school carnivals, family nights, and award/recognition ceremonies. These gatherings often have many photo-worthy moments. If nothing else, you can probably snap a photo of your child with his or her teacher and get a few shots of the classroom as well.**

- **Check with your school's office. Many schools and daycare centers keep cameras on hand for photographing events. Larger schools for older children usually have a yearbook staff as well. Most of these people are likely to be willing to make copies for you—just ask!**

- **Assuming it's okay with your child's teacher, send a disposable camera to school with your child. After a short lesson, your child will likely be able to work the camera with ease. If your child is especially young, ask the teacher if he or she would mind taking a few photos for you.**

PAPER CUTS

One of the biggest issues young photographers face when working with disposable cameras is forgetting to use the flash. Be sure to show your child how to use it, or look forward to a roll of dark photographs.

When you've compiled a decent stack of photographs, sort them out into a few basic categories:

- **Field trips**
- **Outdoor events**
- **Recognitions and events**
- **Daily life in the school routine**
- **Favorite activities**
- **Time with friends**
- **Seasonal and holiday parties**
- **Photos with your child's teacher**
- **Miscellaneous fun photographs and head shots**

(Turn to Appendix B for a worksheet that will help you select which photo categories to use, and keep track of the photographs you have.)

This album is designed to be quick and easy. One to three photographs per category should be more than enough to get you started. And because most of the text in this album consists of hand-written photo captions, there is very little preparation necessary, with two exceptions.

First, conduct a "favorites" interview with your child about the school year you're documenting. Find out what her favorite subject was or what his favorite lunch was. Was there a special field trip? Favorite unit or theme? These are all things you'll want to record. Try finding out your child's favorites:

- **Color**
- **Book**
- **Subject**
- **Creative activity**
- **Sport**
- **Recess game or outdoor activity**
- **Lunch or other school meal/snack**
- **Field trip**
- **Special unit or theme week**

The answers to these questions help provide a glimpse into your child's school life and serve as the foundation for the pages in your album.

Second, see if you can obtain a letter from your child's teacher to include in your child's scrapbook. This provides a fantastic personal touch and will likely be your child's favorite part of the album. If your child's teacher happens to be a scrapbooker, then you're in luck. If not, you can still obtain a personal message from your child's teacher. Try the following:

- **Ask! It certainly can't hurt. Although many teachers have tight schedules, quite a few would be willing to write a quick note to your child.**

- **Many teachers give holiday cards and birthday cards to the children in their class, perhaps most often on Valentine's Day. Consider saving these and using the messages contained in them as part of your child's scrapbook.**

- **Save your child's schoolwork. Teachers often make comments on tests and papers they send home. This can be a great way to keep a record of your child's relationship with his or her teacher.**

Now that you've obtained all the necessary pieces of the puzzle, you're ready to begin creating your album.

GETTING STARTED

To make this fun scrapbook, you'll need the following:

- **5½×8½-inch Office-style album (Preservation Series by SEI)**
- **Assorted 12×12-inch patterned papers from the "Classic Kids" and "Red Wagon" collections (Daisy D's Paper Company)**
- **Metal bookplate (Daisy D's Paper Company)**
- **Alphabet Printed Twill (Creative Impressions)**

- **Several sheets of red and blue flat cardstock**
- **White 8½×11-inch cardstock for computer journaling**
- **Computer for journaling**
- **Paper trimmer, scissors, black pen, adhesive**

This album is fun to embellish and decorate specifically for your child.

Creating this album is quite simple, and it's easy enough to complete in a day. Follow these steps to be on the way to your own educational masterpiece:

1. **Begin by matting all your photos in red or blue cardstock. Because this album doesn't require any special cropping or shaping, it can be easiest to get these out of the way first thing. Save your scraps; you'll be able to use them later.**

2. **Next, cut your patterned paper into 5½×8½-inch blocks. You can get two full pieces out of each sheet of 12×12-inch paper, with extra scraps for creating accents.**

3. **Use the computer to print your page titles. Select your titles according to your photographs, matching them to the categories you selected earlier.**

4. **Create simple cardstock mats for each of your titles, using the scraps left over from step 1.**

5. **Adhere your titles and photos to your patterned paper, using the following layout sketch as a guide.**

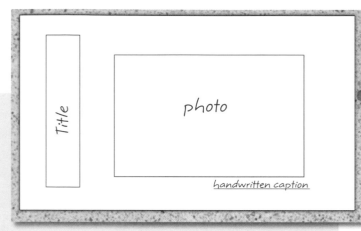

Title

photo

handwritten caption

This sketch shows the placement of your page title, photograph, and caption.

6. **Using a black journaling pen, add a simple caption under each photograph.**

PICTURE THIS

Add additional texture and color to your design by layering an additional patterned paper or two on top of your background sheet before you attach your photographs and page titles.

One of the great things about this album design is that you can create single pages or two-page spreads very easily, depending on the number of photographs you have to work with in each category.

Follow these basic steps to create the remaining pages for your album in all the general categories you selected.

Accomplishments

Star of the Week

Family Fun Night Art Show

This simple page follows the layout guide perfectly.

Notice how easy it is to add a second page to your layout design. Simply skip the title and add another photograph and caption.

Don't forget to include photos from special days at school, such as this outdoor swim day. These photos were taken with a disposable camera sent to school, and they turned out great!

SPECIAL PAGES

Now that you've completed all your basic layouts, it's time to create two extra-special pages you did the legwork for earlier in this chapter.

First is the "School Favorites" page:

1. **Type your child's favorites list and the page title on the computer. Print both on white cardstock.**

2. **Cut out the printed elements, and mat them with red or blue cardstock.**

3. **Adhere these elements to your background pages, along with a favorite photo or two.**

This spread displays a list of the student's favorite things, along with some fun photographs and a handwritten caption.

PICTURE THIS

If your child is able, consider having him write out a list of favorites in his own handwriting—you'll treasure the results.

Finally, you'll want to create a special page or spread containing a letter from your child's teacher. If you obtained this by saving comments or notes sent home on larger sheets of paper, consider using a photocopier to create a reduced size print so you can include the item in your album. (See Chapter 3 for more information on preserving memorabilia in your scrapbooks.)

Create this page in the same way you created your "School Favorites" page, simply substituting the letter in place of the list of favorite items.

This fun page features two memorable photographs along with a note printed and signed on cardstock. I was this child's teacher, so obtaining the letter was a piece of cake!

FINAL STEPS

To complete your album, all you have left to do is decorate the cover. These fun, flat albums were designed to be embellished, so you can really have some fun here. You've already created the interior of your album, so designing the cover to match should be simple.

1. **Start by covering the entire album cover with a sheet of patterned paper.**

2. **Print out a title for your album on the computer, along with a smaller piece that contains the name of the school as well as the year(s) being commemorated.**

3. **Mount your album title on red or blue cardstock, and adhere it to the album.**

4. **Select a favorite horizontal 4×6-inch photo (close-up head shots are great). Mat it with red or blue cardstock, and adhere it to the album.**

5. **Attach the red metal bookplate to the cover using brads or industrial-strength adhesive.**

6. **Place the smaller printout containing the school information inside the bookplate. (For extra security, adhere this paper directly to the cover as well.)**

7. **Wrap the binding in twill tape by wrapping a length of the twill around the entire cover and securing with a knot on the outside of the album.**

You might elect to include a title page in your album as well, but because your cover contains all the information you would normally place here, it's entirely optional.

Congratulations! Your album is now complete, and you have a lasting record of your child's school experience.

PICTURE THIS

Don't have a child? Consider using some of these same techniques and ideas to create an album documenting your own school years, no matter how long ago they might have been. Or if you're a dog owner, consider creating an album to commemorate your pet's experience at obedience school.

MORE TO LEARN

There are many, many additional ways to include school memories in your scrapbooks. Perhaps you just don't have the time to create an entire album, or maybe you want to honor a certain event with a page all its own.

BACK TO SCHOOL

Every fall, going back to school is a huge event and a major milestone. All the stores have fantastic sales, and it seems like it's a chance for everyone to make new beginnings.

Back-to-school layouts can be fun to create—and even more fun to compare over the years. Consider creating a page about one of the following:

- **Shopping for school supplies**
- **How you spent your summer vacation**
- **What changes lie ahead for the coming year**
- **The first day of school**
- **Your school building and classroom**
- **Favorite school memories from the previous year**

This well-designed layout showcases those obligatory first-day-of-school photos perfectly.

(Layout by Michelle Maret)

FIELD TRIPS AND SCHOOL EVENTS

Perhaps some of the best school-related memories are the ones that happen outside the classroom. Class trips, school dances, and carnivals are just a few of the events worth showing off in your albums.

This fun layout captures the excitement and emotion of heading out on a field trip for the first time.

(Layout by Sue Rhinehart)

If you're able to chaperone an event, be sure to take along your camera to capture the moment. Consider printing duplicate photographs for other parents, or post the photos online. Other parents who aren't able to attend will appreciate your thoughtfulness.

The annual homecoming dance is an exciting event for many high school girls. The emotion and beauty of the event are captured beautifully in this layout.

(Layout by Kelly Edgerton)

GRADUATION CEREMONIES

If there were ever a school event worth scrapbooking, graduation would be it. Graduations mark a major life change. Whether it's moving from preschool to elementary school, high school to college, or college to the "real world," graduating is as much about creating a new beginning as it is celebrating an ending.

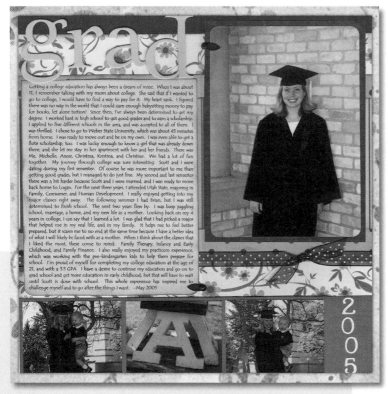

This touching layout reveals the emotion of the artist upon her college graduation—a long-awaited and hard-earned victory.

(Layout by Heather Taylor)

Preschool graduations can be as exciting as ones that come later on in the educational experience. For this mother, graduation was a touching moment—her daughter, finally ready to start kindergarten.

(Layout by Marie Cox)

Emotions run high at graduation time, and not just for the graduate. If you're watching your child or another loved one finish school, consider creating a page expressing your feelings on the event, as well as your wishes and hopes for the graduate's future.

LESSONS LEARNED

More than anything else, education is about learning. The large events, the ceremonies, the field trips—it all boils down to one thing: getting the information and experiences necessary to be productive and happy later in life.

Some lessons are found in textbooks; others are not. Try creating a page celebrating the lessons learned in your own school experience, and be sure to document your children's discoveries as well.

Sometimes, applying the strategies learned in school to life at home is all you need to do to solve the problem at hand—in this case, making slushies!

(Layout by Alecia Ackerman Grimm)

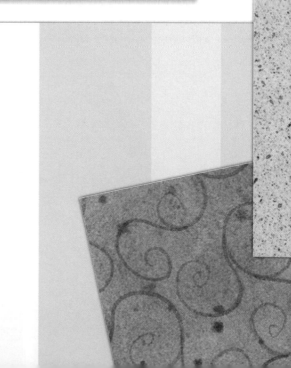

THE LEAST YOU NEED TO KNOW

- Creating an album to document a year in the life of a child's school experience can be meaningful and fun.

- There are many ways to obtain photographs of your child at school. Consider sending a disposable camera to school with your child for an easy and cost-effective solution.

- Be sure to include events such as school dances, field trips, and carnivals in your scrapbooks.

- When scrapbooking graduations and other emotion-packed events, be sure to describe your feelings on your scrapbook pages.

- Lessons learned—both inside and outside the classroom—are some of the most important ones to remember and include in your scrapbook albums.

IN THIS CHAPTER:

- Creating an album to celebrate the athletic accomplishments of an individual or team

- Creative ways to scrap-book action photos

- Fun page ideas for games and everyday activities

Chapter 8

Go Team! The Sports Album

Sports are a natural part of life. Whether you're the star athlete or simply an enthusiastic spectator, chances are, sports have impacted your life in one way or another.

When you're the athlete, it can be easy to constantly be focused on the future. There's always another meet to prepare for, another game to begin strategizing for. It's important to take a moment to remember your past accomplishments, though, and celebrate the journey you've taken so far in the sport.

Whether the star athlete is you or your child, this album is the perfect project to help you highlight your sporting memories.

Dane,

I didn't know how much I would love being the Mother to a son until I had you. While there are occasionally still quiet, loving and tender moments, you are all about overwhelming energy and a constant need to be in motion! I guess that's what being a boy is all about and I am learning to enjoy it. Watching you spin round and round on this tire swing was enough to turn my stomach but you could have gone on

KEEPING IT REAL

This album project is designed to help you cele-brate your (or someone else's) journey through a particular sport. You likely have piles of sports photographs just waiting to be included in a special album. If so, this scrapbook project is for you.

CREATING YOUR ALBUM

Unlike many of the projects you've worked on so far, this album does not require a lot of advance planning or the use of a worksheet or preprinted journaling. And because this project is designed to work with 4×6-inch photographs, you don't even need to print out your photos in any certain way. Simply grab your stack of photographs, and you're ready to begin.

In addition to your photographs, you'll need to collect a few supplies:

- **11×8½-inch post-bound album (Maple Lane Press by EK Success)**

- **Fuzzy alphabet stickers in a coordinating color (Creative Imaginations)**

- **12×12-inch patterned and solid paper collection with coordinating stickers (Tennis Anyone by Arctic Frog)**

- **8½×11-inch white cardstock, several sheets**

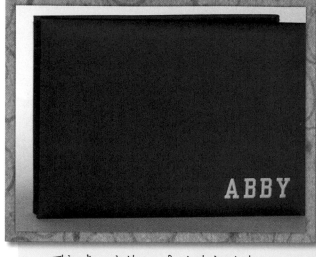

This album is the perfect choice to house your collection of athletic memories.

Creating your album is simple and easy. Start by creating a title page:

1. **Select a piece of patterned paper, and cut it to 11×8½ inches.**

2. **Cut a coordinating solid paper to 9×6½ inches. Mount on the center of your patterned paper.**

3. **Add a favorite 4×6-inch photo, vertically oriented.**

4. **Using alphabet stickers from the Arctic Frog collection, add a title to your page.**

5. **Add the athlete's name using additional alphabet stickers. If desired, add a few more stickers for visual interest.**

PICTURE THIS

If blue and yellow don't work with your photographs (or happen to be the official colors of a rival school), try a different paper collection. Visit www.arcticfrog.com for many more choices.

This simple title page sets the stage for your album

Sports Memories

ABBY

After you've created your title page, you'll want to begin work on the interior pages of your album. There are two basic page designs for this project, one for horizontally oriented photographs, and one for vertically oriented photographs.

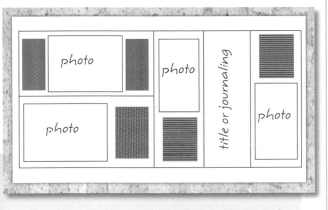

These page designs are the foundation for your album.

Creating your album's interior pages is easier than it might seem at first. To create a horizontally oriented page, follow these steps:

1. **Cut a piece of paper 11×4¼ inches from two different contrasting solids.**

2. **Adhere them to a sheet of plain white cardstock, one across the top and one at the bottom, so the entire page is covered.**

3. **Add your photographs to the page, as shown on the layout sketch.**

4. **Add smaller blocks of patterned paper on each side of your photos. These don't have to be measured exactly. It's easiest to cut a strip of paper 4¼ inches high and simply trim off the length you need.**

5. **If desired, add stickers to accent.**

This page design effectively showcases the photographs it features.

PAPER **C**UTS

Just because you don't have to plan this project ahead of time, don't let that be an excuse for sloppy work or mismatched pages. Choose photographs that complement each other to include on each page.

Creating a page for vertically oriented photos is just as easy:

1. **Cut a sheet of solid-colored paper to 11×8½ inches.**

2. **Cut two strips of paper measuring 4½8½ inches from a contrasting solid.**

3. **Adhere the strips to your larger page, one on each end.**

4. **Add your photographs, one on each side.**

5. **Fill in the remaining space with patterned paper blocks, using the same method you used for the page featuring horizontal photographs.**

6. **Add a title or journaling in the center of the page.**

This page features an inspiring title in the center.
If you want, substitute journaling about the event
pictured in place of the page title.

PICTURE THIS

Inspirational quotes make great additions to sports albums.
Visit www.quoteland.com for a fantastic variety.

One of the best things about this album is that there doesn't have to be an end! You can add as many pages as you like, until you've included all your photographs. You can even leave empty space in the back to add photographs from future events at a later date.

WANT TO INCLUDE MORE?

Your sports photographs are the highlight of the album you just created. But perhaps you'd like to include a little something more in your album. Try one of these great ideas to create a truly memorable keepsake:

- **Include copies of newspaper clippings related to your sport.**

- **Include a photograph of a medal or trophy in your album.**

- **Include a list of your top 10 favorite moments as an athlete.**

- **Create a timeline showcasing your participation and growth in the sport.**

- **Add an autograph section, and have fellow athletes and coaches add their signatures to the album.**

No matter how you choose to personalize it, you're sure to end up with a sports album you can truly cherish and enjoy for years to come.

CELEBRATING SPORTS IN OTHER WAYS

Only have a handful of sports photos? Perhaps you'd like a way to scrapbook your child's one week as a ballet dancer, or maybe just get a few ideas for clever ways to include action shots in your albums. Either way, I've got you covered.

TRADITIONAL SPORTS MEMORIES

There are two common types of sports photographs. First up is the posed portrait shot. There are many ways to scrapbook this type of photograph, but what's most important is to let the photograph take center stage as the focus of the page. Try one of these ideas:

- **Use the athlete's number as a page title.**

- **Create a list of the athlete's accomplishments that season and pair it with the photograph.**

- **Include your athlete's official statistics (height, weight, etc.) as part of the scrapbook page.**

This simply designed layout allows the photograph to truly shine. Notice how the athlete's number is used for the title of the page, while his name and the year are handwritten in the bottom left corner.

The second most common type of sports photograph is the team action shot. These shots are fun and exciting to work with but often pose their own challenges due to the fact that they're generally taken from a distance and might suffer from poor lighting or blurry activity. Don't let that deter you from scrapbooking these important photographs. Try one of these ideas for your next layout:

- **Create a photo montage, using several different photographs to cover your entire background page.**

- **Enlarge a single photo and lighten it. Print it out and use it as the backdrop for your page.**

- **Use one or two of these photographs and let your journaling take center stage on your layout.**

This fun page accurately reflects the mood of the photographs: bold, intense, and quite a lot of fun!

(Layout by Becky Lynn Teichmiller)

This stunning page shows father and son enjoying the same sport, years apart.

(Layout by Sheredian Vickers, Scrapjazz.com design team)

PICTURE THIS

Your entire journey in sports is worthy of scrapbooking. Try a "then and now" page to show growth and change in a sport.

EVERYDAY ACTION

Action photos aren't just a result of the highly athletic. Many different life moments, particularly those involving children, lend themselves to fun and unique action photographs. Consider the following subjects:

- **A child on a swing or one jumping on or off of just about anything**

- **A newly married couple on the dance floor**

- **An elderly couple laughing hysterically at a joke**

All these situations can lead to action photography. Knowing how to use these photos effectively on a scrapbook page is important.

When selecting products for pages and projects using action photos, think about the mood you're trying to convey. Chances are, subdued hues and soft pastels aren't going to be the right choice. Opt for products that can contribute to the idea of motion and action as well as the action being portrayed.

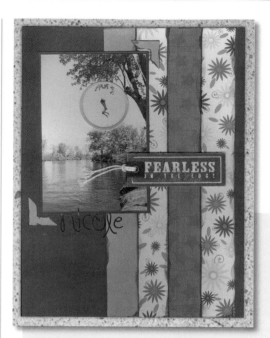

Notice how the artist highlights the action in the photograph by using a metal ring to focus the viewer's eye.

(Layout by Rachael Giallongo)

FUN AND GAMES

Sometimes, the sports in your life aren't high impact. Anything from a weekly poker game to a ride at the fair can be considered a sporting event. When it comes to your scrapbooks, don't forget to include these pieces of everyday sportsmanship. Consider creating a layout about one of the following:

- **Your favorite board game**

- **Your favorite outdoor games as a child (e.g., Kick the Can)**

- **"Mental sports" you enjoy (crossword puzzles, trivia games, etc.)**

- **Favorite sports to watch and favorite sports teams**

- **Life as a professional athlete: if you could take the place of any pro athlete for the day, who would you pick? Why?**

Try using a series of action photographs to portray your subject's personality.

(Layout by Rachael Giallongo)

HOW TO Hula hoop

June 25, 2000
Borden Family Fun Day

This hilarious page shows the viewer the steps of successful hula hooping, a timeless pastime.

(Layout by Kim Brown)

CARD SHARKS

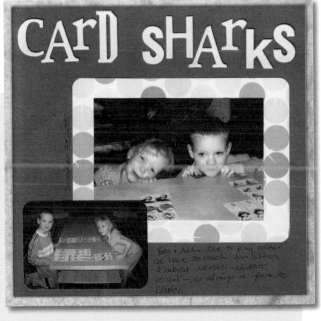

This fun page shows two children playing their favorite game: Memory.

THE LEAST YOU NEED TO KNOW

- Creating an album to showcase your sports photographs is easy and fun.

- There are many unique ways to include sports photos in your traditional scrapbooks.

- Action photos come from many of life's everyday moments. Don't be afraid to include these in your albums.

- Scrapbook pages about games, activities, and favorite sports can be unique additions to your albums.

VOTE

Dad,

I've never been a parent ... so perhaps I'm wrong abou... But it ... me that ... mes. There's ... much to teach your children, and no real way to know

All those times we talked about goals and priorities, I was paying attention. (Even if it didn't seem like it.) And I was paying attention plenty of other times as well — there

Part 3

Celebrating Your Relationships

Scrapbooking events is probably the most common reason beginners decide to scrapbook, but it doesn't end there! Relationships—whether romantic, family, or friendly—shape our lives and determine who we spend them with. Celebrating someone you care about in a special album is a fantastic and special way to preserve that relationship on paper.

Whether you choose to remember the life of someone who is no longer with you, create a tribute to your partner, or simply create an album celebrating a special friendship—these projects help you quickly and easily make a lasting keepsake honoring someone you care about. If possible, be sure to share your final project with its subject. If you can bear to part with them, these albums make fantastic gifts!

IN THIS CHAPTER:

- Creating an album based on the music you love to celebrate your relationship with your significant other

- Downloading the songs you cherish and burning them to a compact disc

- Fantastic scrapbook page ideas or weddings, anniversaries, and other special moments

- Journaling starters to help you capture your most intimate feelings on paper

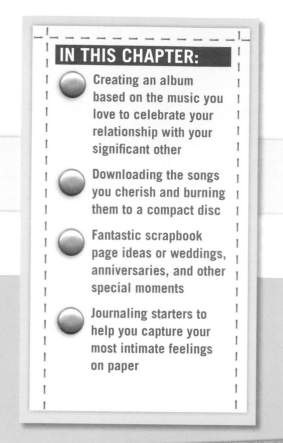

*My Partner, my best friend
all my Dreams come true
everything I could want
I found in Loving
YOU*

She simply can't imagine what her life would be like without him. Mostly though she wants to

Chapter 9

Your Songs: A Musical Mini-Album Celebrating Your Significant Other

Few relationships are as emotionally charged as the romantic relationships that define our lives. No matter what stage of life you're in, or how long you've been with your special someone, or even if you're choosing to remember a relationship from your past, you have a story to tell. From the moment you met to the first dance at your wedding, the birth of your child to that fantastic dinner you shared last week—all these are times worth celebrating. Why not celebrate them through song in a beautiful, vintage-inspired scrapbook?

DREAM come true

It is such a "little girl" dream...to grow up, fall in love, get married, and live happily ever after. How strange it all seems when it finally comes true. As a young girl, I never could have dreamed up a better guy. Dan is so amazing in so many ways and on so many different levels—

I can't believe that in just under a year, I'll be calling myself his wife. I consider myself blessed every day that I found

SETTING YOUR STORY TO SONGS

Creating a scrapbook set to music is a fun and exciting way to tell the story of your relationship with your significant other. Think back to the first time you met your special someone. Was there a song playing in the background? What about the first song you danced to at your wedding reception? Chances are, you associate many songs with these special memories. In this project, you'll take those songs and combine them with memorable photographs to create a one-of-a-kind keepsake album.

S C R A P   F A C T

Telling stories through music isn't a new concept. For hundreds of years, individuals have been combining the art of storytelling with the art of songwriting; this evolved into the music you hear on the radio today.

GETTING STARTED

The first step in creating your album is to make a list of the songs you want to include. Select 8 to 15 songs, one that represents each stage in your relationship. (Appendix B contains a worksheet to help you select each of your songs and plan your album.) You might want to begin with a song describing each of you as individuals and then move on to select a song for each stage of your relationship. The progression of every relationship is different, but consider the following general timeline as a starting point for your album:

PICTURE THIS

Don't have a significant other, or just want to create this project with a different spin? Try making this album for a friend or family member. Follow the same format, choosing songs that mean the most to you. This album can be a great gift for anyone you care about.

Song 1: A song about you.

Song 2: A song about your significant other.

Song 3: A song from when you first met.

Song 4: A song from the early stages of your relationship, when you fell in love.

Song 5: A song (or perhaps two) celebrating the ways in which you express love.

Song 6: A song from your wedding day.

Song 7: A song that expresses how you felt after making it through a difficult time together or after a rough spot in your relationship.

Song 8: A song showcasing your emotions after having a child.

Song 9: A song that expresses how you feel about your significant other right now.

Song 10: A song looking ahead to the future.

Of course, everyone's outline will be different. If you aren't yet married or don't have any children, include more songs from the earlier stages of your relationship. Celebrating your fiftieth wedding anniversary? Choose songs that share your emotions upon the marriages of your own children and the birth of your grandchildren.

Don't forget to include songs that highlight special moments and memories unique to the two of you. Be sure to add any additional songs that are on your list of favorites as well.

After you've chosen your songs, select a photo or two from your collection to accompany each song. You'll likely want to make copies of your photos for this project. Because the completed album is only 6×6 inches, wallet- or similar-size prints are ideal for this project. Be sure to select an additional photo or two for your opening and closing pages.

Finally, decide on a title for your album. "The Story of Us" is a popular choice. You could also elect to use the title of one of the songs contained in your scrapbook.

BEGINNING YOUR ALBUM

To make this fun album, you'll need the following:

- 6×6-inch Post-bound, gatefold album (Life's Journey by K&Company)

- Assorted vintage-style and artistic 12×12-inch patterned papers (Creative Imaginations, K&Company, Leaving Prints, Rusty Pickle)

- Vintage images and quotes (ArtChix Studio, Crafty Secrets)

- Several sheets of 8½×11-inch ivory-colored cardstock

- Assorted ribbons (Creative Impressions, May Arts)

- Dye ink pads in two coordinating vintage colors

- Small alphabet stickers (Crafty Secrets)

- Computer for journaling and burning CD

- Blank recordable CD, white CD label, CD envelope

- Paper trimmer, scissors, black pen, adhesive

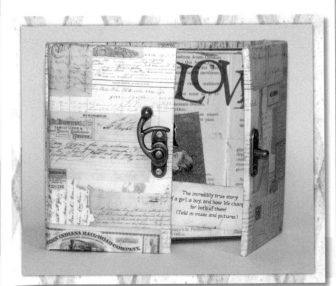

Now that you have all your supplies gathered and your music and photographs selected, you're ready to start creating your album. It's easiest to begin by using a computer to produce your journaling blocks.

Creating the text for this album is simple. You'll need to make two journaling blocks for each spread, as well as one each for your title and closing pages. (See Chapter 1 if you need assistance with this.)

The first style of journaling block you create is the song information block. On the first line, include the number of the song (according to your timeline), the title of the song, and the artist's name. If you want, include a second line containing the name(s) of the songwriter(s). Create one of these blocks for each song you've chosen.

The second style of journaling block you need is the story block. For each of these, simply type out a few sentences about why the song is meaningful to you and how it relates to the story of your relationship. Again, you'll want one of these for each of your songs.

This spread's journaling blocks are easy to read and tell the story perfectly.

This gorgeous scrapbook is the perfect setting for your musical album.

Start by gathering recordings of all the songs you plan to include. You'll want to include the same songs you included in your album, in the same order. If you don't already own all of the songs on CDs, try using an online service such as iTunes (www.itunes.com) to purchase your songs and download them to your computer.

PAPER CUTS

Many online services and programs appear to offer music downloads for free. Beware that these sites are usually offering their material illegally. Be sure to honor copyright laws and uphold your integrity by purchasing your music from a reputable source.

After you have all your songs gathered, you're ready to burn them to your blank CD. Depending on the type of computer and software available to you, the steps for this process vary. Follow the directions included with your software to create your CD. If you used iTunes or a similar program to download your songs, check for help online. Many of these programs and services have the ability to record CDs directly.

After you've created your CD, you want to create a label so your CD matches your album. Take an ink pad and turn it upside down. Brush the surface of the pad firmly across the label, repeating until the entire surface of the label is completely covered

with color. Finally, add a title to your label using small letter stickers.

To create a pocket for your CD, take your CD envelope and remove the top flap. Then, color the envelope in the same way you colored the label, using a coordinating ink color.

Mount the pocket on the back inside cover of the album using a strong adhesive. Add your CD, and your album is now truly complete.

This CD looks great at the back of this album. Now the reader of the scrapbook can follow along with the music—the best part of the album.

Your musical album will be a keepsake to cherish for many years to come. It will serve as a reminder of your love should you encounter difficult times, and be a testimony of your love to celebrate during the good ones.

CELEBRATING LOVE

Do you want to highlight romantic relationships in your standard-size scrapbooks? Perhaps you're in a very new relationship and just want to make a scrapbook page commemorating your first date. Or maybe you just attended the wedding of a close friend and want to create a simple page to record the event. There are lots of ways to include these relationships in your regular albums.

WEDDINGS

Weddings are popular events to document in scrapbooks. Weddings are generally fun and emotional occasions that result in quite a few photographs. There are so many ways to include weddings in your scrapbooks.

If you were a guest at a recent wedding, try creating a two-page spread capturing the highlights. Include photographs of the happy couple, the wedding party, the cake, and a select group of guests. The result will be a gorgeous layout capturing the fun and emotion of the day.

This beautiful layout highlights this couple's unique wedding cake, as well as other memorable moments of the day.

(Layout by Amanda Bohall)

It you were a participant in a wedding—perhaps even the bride or groom—you'll likely have even more photographs to work with. Try creating single pages or spreads focusing on one or two specific details. Combine all these pages into a full-size album for a truly unique wedding keepsake. When selecting the pages to create, consider the following details of the wedding:

- **The bride or groom getting ready for the ceremony**

- **The bride and groom with their attendants**

- **The first kiss as husband and wife**

- **The bride and groom leaving the church**

- **The bride and groom in the receiving line**

- **The bride and groom with their siblings and parents**

- **The best man's toast**

- **Cutting the cake**

- **The first dance for the bride and groom, as well as any other special dances (the bride with her father, etc.)**

- **Tossing of the bouquet and garter**

- **The couple's exit for their honeymoon**

Of course, many memorable moments occur throughout the course of a typical wedding. Be sure to include those that mean the most to you, along with photos of everyone who was a part of the special day.

This beautiful layout captures the first kiss of the bride and groom perfectly. Notice how the bright colors and fun patterns help portray the excitement and passion of the moment.

(Layout by Linda Harrison)

CELEBRATING YOUR SIGNIFICANT OTHER

Why not create a scrapbook page detailing the things you love about your significant other? Try making a page centered around one of the following themes:

- **Ten Things I Love About You.**

- **Reasons I Said "Yes"** (in response to a marriage proposal).

- **Choose one or two specific personality traits and create a page about them. (Try making several and including them in an album of their own!)**

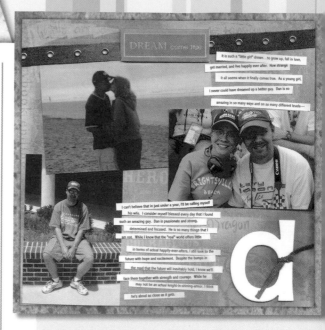

This layout reflects on the possibility of a "real" knight in shining armor. So many women feel this way about their men—why not celebrate it on a scrapbook page?

This fun layout showcases the subject's fun side, and the heartfelt journaling expresses exactly how the artist feels.

(Layout by Teresa Olier)

For another fun page, try creating a layout that enables you to reflect on the time you've spent with your significant other. No matter what stage of life you're in, capturing your emotions on paper is an important and worthwhile process.

This beautiful page reflects on the emotions of the couple approaching their tenth year together. This simple and effective design keeps the focus on the words and photographs—perfectly designed.

(Layout by Marie Cox)

EVERYDAY MOMENTS TOGETHER

Chances are, you've spent plenty of time with your significant other—especially if you're married. You've taken trips together, attended events, and celebrated anniversaries. You've likely already scrapbooked your vacations and other more defined moments together, but don't forget to include those "everyday" moments in the pages of your scrapbook albums as well.

Consider creating a scrapbook page about one of the following:

- **A favorite local location to visit**
- **Your nicknames for each other**
- **How you met**
- **Favorite activities together**
- **Time spent with your families**
- **Your everyday "routines" as a couple**
- **Your similarities and differences**

This fun layout showcases the favorite things of both halves of the relationship, in their own handwriting. Consider asking your significant other to provide some handwritten journaling for one of your pages.

No matter how you choose to include your romantic relationships—and the relationships of others you love—in your scrapbooks, you'll be glad you did. Who we choose to spend our lives with says a lot about each of us as individuals. Be sure to celebrate this in your albums.

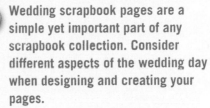

THE LEAST YOU NEED TO KNOW

- Creating a vintage-style scrapbook to celebrate your story as a couple is an easy and fun project.

- Including a CD of your favorite songs provides the perfect musical touch.

- Wedding scrapbook pages are a simple yet important part of any scrapbook collection. Consider different aspects of the wedding day when designing and creating your pages.

- Be sure to celebrate the person you love in your scrapbooks. Design pages showcasing the different stages in your relationship and the emotions you've felt along the way.

IN THIS CHAPTER:

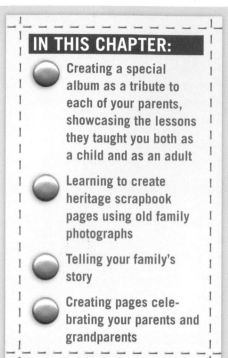

- Creating a special album as a tribute to each of your parents, showcasing the lessons they taught you both as a child and as an adult

- Learning to create heritage scrapbook pages using old family photographs

- Telling your family's story

- Creating pages celebrating your parents and grandparents

high expectations

Chapter 10

Lessons Learned: A Tribute to Your Parents

Parents are unlike anyone else in our lives. As young children, we count on them to meet our every need. As teenagers, we firmly believe the opposite of every piece of advice they try to give us. As adults, after we are free to live our own lives, we finally realize how much wisdom our parents actually have.

So often, though, our parents don't necessarily get to hear how much they mean to us. Sure, we tell our parents we love them. But when was the last time you were able to sit down with your parents and let them know exactly what about them you admire and respect, and what you appreciate about the lessons they've taught you?

Creating this album is your chance to do exactly that. You can choose to create a scrapbook for your mother, your father, or any other person who has had significant impact on your life. The result is an album commemorating your experiences together and celebrating the things they've taught you. It's a gift any parent will truly love.

PICTURE THIS

If your parent is no longer living or is currently estranged from your family, don't let that stop you from creating a scrapbook sharing what he or she still means to you. Even if you keep it for yourself, this album is still a fun and meaningful project to create.

because of you

LOVE

CREATING YOUR SCRAPBOOKS

This project is very dear to my heart. After coming into my own as an adult, I've searched for years for a way to let my parents know what they mean to me and how much I appreciate the things they've taught me. When I came up with this project, I knew I'd found the answer. I elected to create a pair of matching albums, one in shades of blue for my mother, and a second in shades of green for my father. Whether you choose to create one album or an entire set, this project is truly an experience you'll value.

GETTING STARTED

This album takes a considerable amount of planning, so you'll likely want to turn to the Album Planning Worksheet in Appendix B right away to help you get started.

First, you'll want to spend some time naming the lessons your parents have taught you. This could be anything from clichés, such as "A penny saved is a penny earned," to incredibly specific advice, such as what brand of cars to purchase. Every lesson has a story, and these are the ones you'll want to preserve in your album. The album we're working

with has 20 pages, so you have plenty of room to include a significant amount of lessons learned.

After you've listed your lessons, you'll need to gather the photographs to complement them. This can be the tricky part. For each lesson, try to find an older photo that features your parent at a young age, as well as ones of yourself learning that same lesson. You'll also want to select two photos for the cover of your album: one older photo of your parent and another of your parent and you together.

After you've listed your lessons and gathered your photographs, it's time to begin creating your album.

PAPER CUTS

Because you're working with older photos that might be significant to your entire family, making copies of the originals and using those in your album is highly recommended. You don't want to end up destroying the only copy of a special photograph just because your paper trimmer slips!

One of the most important lessons my mother taught me was "first things first." This was her mantra for me throughout high school and college, helping me stay focused on the tasks at hand. I paired photos from my high school and college graduations with this fun one of my mother in her own college dorm room.

BEGINNING YOUR PROJECT

To create this special album, begin by gathering all the materials you'll need:

- **7×7-inch spiral scrapbook album (7gypsies)**

- **Patterned paper and coordinating tags (Melissa Frances)**

- **Rub-on letters ("Beach" by Making Memories, "Portobello Road" by 7gypsies)**

- **Scallop tag die and die cutting system (Sizzix)**

- **Ivory-colored cardstock**

- **Assorted ribbon (Offray)**

- **Paper trimmer, adhesive, and black journaling pen**

This beautiful album is easy to create and lovely to look at.

After you've gathered your supplies, it's time to begin working on your album's interior pages.

Begin by opening your album to the first page. Because this project begins with a 2-page spread, simply adhere the front page to the inside front cover of the album. Be sure to use a strong, dry-based adhesive so the page won't become loose over time. After you've glued your page to the cover, your album will open to a 2-page layout.

This first layout is slightly different from the rest of the book. On these 2 pages, you introduce your album's concept. I chose to do this in the form of a letter to each of my parents, explaining why I was creating the album: to celebrate all the things they'd taught me through the years. You can elect to do your introduction pages in a more traditional way, or design them any other way you'd like.

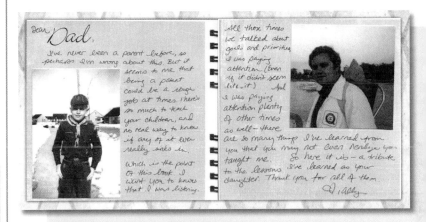

This spread contains a letter to my father introducing the album and also features a few special photographs from his childhood as well as my own.

After you've created your introduction, turn the page, and you're ready to add layouts featuring the lessons your parent has taught you. The layout design for these 2-page spreads is quite simple.

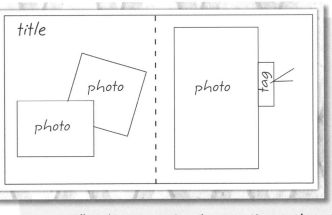

Follow this easy design when creating your layouts.

To create each of your interior spreads, complete the following steps:

1. **Cut two matching sheets of patterned paper to 7×7 inches, and adhere these to the blank pages in your album.**

2. **Use the rub-on letters to write out the page's title, which should be the name of the lesson you're describing. If you'd like, place your title on ivory cardstock before adding it to your page.**

3. **Using the Sizzix die cutting system, cut a tag from ivory cardstock.**

4. **Add journaling to the tag using a journaling pen. Be sure to explain how you learned the lesson, why it was important to you, and what it means to you today. Feel free to write on both sides of the tag.**

5. **Attach a small length of ribbon to the end of the tag, by either tying it on or using a stapler.**

6. **Place your photographs on your layout as shown in the sketch. If you have more or fewer photos than the sketch shows, simply add or omit them as needed. When attaching your largest photo, only apply adhesive to three sides of the photograph, leaving one side completely open.**

7. **Insert your tag behind your photo on the open edge so it can be removed for reading.**

8. **If you want, add date information to your photographs using the small rub-on letters.**

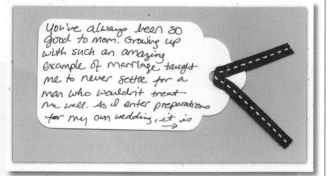

This tag contains just the right amount of journaling and is ready to add to its corresponding layout.

This spread is fully complete, sharing the lesson of "set high expectations." By watching the amazing way my father consistently loved my mother throughout their marriage, he taught me to never settle for anything less than total, pure love.

Simply repeat this process for each lesson you'd like to include in your album. When you've added all the spreads you've planned, your album is almost complete.

FINISHING TOUCHES

Now it's time to decorate the cover of your album. Begin by cutting a sheet of patterned paper to 7×7 inches and adhering it to your album's cover. Next, add your title and the pair of photographs you selected during your album preparation. Add any small embellishments you want to include. End by tying a small strip of ribbon on each ring of your album's spiral. This adds a fun, vintage look to your album.

Your album's cover is up to you. There's no set of rules or expectations. Feel free to design it however you'd like, or copy the example shown earlier.

This album is uniquely personal, so don't be afraid to deviate from the design shown here to meet your own personal needs. You could even try creating a single album for both of your parents and giving it to them together. However you decide to create this special album, you won't regret that you did—and neither will your parents.

SCRAPBOOKING YOUR MENTORS

Parents are just one of the many groups of people who help shape us from children into adults. Grandparents, godparents, teachers, and even friends and neighbors can fall into this category, too. Creating an entire album for each person who has impacted your life over the years would become very time-consuming! Why not try creating a single scrapbook page to celebrate another important individual in your life?

GIVING THANKS

Expressing gratitude is one of the primary reasons you'll likely want to create a page honoring a special mentor. There are many ways to do this in your scrapbooks. Try one of these ideas:

- **Consider creating a scrapbook page about what your mentor means to you and why you are glad he or she is a part of your life.**

- **Create a layout showcasing a fun part of your parent or grandparent's personality. Explain why it strikes you so much.**

- **In the case of parents and grandparents, try creating a scrapbook page detailing the traits you believe you inherited from each of them.**

This heartwarming layout features the artist's reflections about her grandfather and how he was the central male role model in her life.

(Layout by April Derrick)

A mother's house often tells you a lot about the woman who runs it. This layout captures the color and mood of the home of the artist's own mother, while revealing a little about her character at the same time.

(Layout by Andrea Steed, co-founder, Scrapjazz.com)

Grandparents are indeed something to be thankful for. This layout showcases that gratitude just perfectly.

(Layout by Monica Schoenemann)

WRITING A LETTER

Whether your parent or role model is currently living or is no longer with you, sometimes writing a letter can be the perfect way to let them know that you care, tell them how they shaped your life, and thank them for all they've done for you.

Try writing a letter to your own role model and featuring it on a scrapbook page. Whether you have a lot to say or simply just want to say thanks, directly addressing the subject of your scrapbook page provides a different approach to your journaling and results in a truly unique page to include in your scrapbook albums.

On this gorgeous layout, the artist captures a few reasons to thank her mother for a job well done.

(Layout by Alexis Hardy)

Writing a letter to a parent or special mentor in your life can be a fun and rewarding process. If your parent is no longer living, it can also be an exercise in healing to help aid you in your grieving and give you an opportunity to remember how much your parent meant to you.

WORKING WITH HERITAGE PHOTOGRAPHS

Of course, it has been fun incorporating old photographs with new ones and seeing the combination result in some truly beautiful art. But sometimes, all you have is old photographs. Perhaps you have a name and a date to match; perhaps you have no information at all except that somehow, sometime, this particular person was related to you. Try one or more of the following ideas when working with old photographs:

- **If you only have a name and a date, include that with your photographs. Try using a simple layout design to keep the emphasis on the photographs.**

- **Match your layout design to the era of the photographs: use everything from ribbons and lace for the early 1900s to retro patterns for photos from the 1970s.**

- **Don't have any information to go with your photos? Make it up! Create a layout about what you think these people might be thinking about, what their names might have been, and more. Be sure to include a note somewhere on the layout that the information you've included is fictional—you don't want to confuse future generations!**

- **Be sure to use only acid-free products when working with heritage photographs, especially if you're working with originals.**

This layout contains a heartfelt letter from the artist to her deceased mother, thanking her for the example of faith she set during her lifetime. The artist shares how that example has helped shape her life today.

(Layout by Rachael Giallongo)

*Portrait of
Martha Hamburg*

Hair of silk

Eyes of chocolate

Skin like cream

Cheeks of apples

Lips of cherries

Teeth like pearls

This beautiful layout is perfectly composed. The page elements match the photograph wonderfully, with just the right amount of text.

(Layout by Pam Callaghan)

This layout is well designed and perfectly matched to these 1970s photographs.

(Layout by Rachael Giallongo)

THE LEAST YOU NEED TO KNOW

- Creating a scrapbook full of the lessons your parents have taught you is an ideal way to pay tribute to their love while at the same time making a special gift for them to enjoy.

- When working with heritage photographs, it's a good idea to make copies of the originals before including them in your scrapbook art.

- Making a scrapbook page to thank a special mentor in your life is a fantastic way to express gratitude through art. Try adding a letter to your subject as part of your page's journaling.

- Heritage photos present unique challenges in scrapbooking. Don't be afraid to skimp on the journaling if you don't have the details; or if you should so desire, create your own fictional account using your old family photographs.

IN THIS CHAPTER:

- Creating an accordion album for a close friend

- Writing letters and lists to preserve your best friendship memories

- Fabulous ideas for celebrating your friendships in your traditional scrapbooks

Chapter 11

Friends Are Forever: An Accordion Album for Your Best Friend

Friendships are some of the most important relationships in every person's life. Whether your best friends are male or female, adult or child, they are worth documenting. The high points, the low points, and those oh-so-silly points are all important to include and remember. Why not create a special scrapbook for an important friend in your life? The accordion album shown in this chapter is an ideal fit.

THE PERFECT TRIBUTE

It's the perfect birthday gift—a fun, *accordion album* full of photos, memories, and a special letter from you to your friend. Best of all? This album project is easy enough to create in just a few hours but meaningful enough to be treasured for a lifetime.

SCRAP SPEAK

An **accordion album** is a scrapbook made of a single length of paper, folded multiple times in opposite directions to create several panels. These panels then serve as the pages of the album.

GETTING STARTED

Unlike many projects, this album doesn't require much preparation. Start by gathering a pile of 4×6-inch photos of you and your friend. There's no set number required; try to aim for at least 8 but no more than 16.

Two basic journaling components are required for this project: a series of five lists, as well as a personal letter to your friend that runs throughout the album. Because these are handwritten, you might want to just create these as you go along. If you're nervous about writing directly on the album before you've planned out your wording, try composing your journaling ahead of time so you can simply copy it onto the finished album. This ensures that you're able to include everything you want to say and also helps you avoid mistakes when it comes time to add your journaling to the album. (Turn to Appendix B for a worksheet to assist you with this process.)

After you've prepared your journaling (if you want) and gathered your photos, you're ready to begin creating your album.

SCRAP FACT

Accordion books have been around for centuries. They were originally used for religious texts nearly 1,000 years ago. Since then, the accordion has evolved into a common structure for both publishers and book artists.

MAKING THE ALBUM

To create this fun project, you'll need the following supplies:

- **Accordion Keeper Album (Bazzill Basics)**
- **12×12-inch cardstock sheets (Bazzill Basics)**
- **Large monogram letter (Outrageous Daisy)**
- **Mini Library Pockets, Mini File Folders, Mini Cardstock Envelopes (Outrageous Daisy)**
- **Black rub-on letters (Heidi Grace Designs)**
- **White rub-on letters (Wordsworth)**
- **Paper trimmer, scissors, black pen, adhesive**

This fun and colorful project is the perfect gift for your best friend.

Creating this fun album is quick and easy. Follow these simple steps to make your own masterpiece:

1. **Begin by cropping and matting your photos using the textured cardstock sheets. A simple border of about ¼ inch provides the perfect touch. It's fun to leave some photos at full size, but cut at least five of them slightly smaller.**

2. **Adhere the photos to various panels in your accordion, placing one photo per panel. Skip every other panel or so, leaving at least four total panels blank.**

PAPER CUTS

Don't forget that accordion albums are double-sided. Be sure you add photos and text to both sides of the accordion so your final product won't have any blank spaces.

This matted photo is the perfect start for this panel of the accordion.

3. **Next, select a combination of five mini library pockets, file folders, and envelopes. Adhere these accents, one per panel, on the same panels as your smaller matted photographs.**

4. **Using black rub-on letters, add a title to each of your accents. For my album, I chose:**

   - **Remember the Time …**
   - **Favorite Moments**
   - **I Never Told You**
   - **Funniest Memories**
   - **I Admire You Because …**

This panel is now ready to go.

5. **Now it's time to pick up your journaling pen. Open each of the accents and create a list inside each one that corresponds to the title on the outside. For example, inside my "I Admire You Because …" file folder, I wrote a list of five things I truly respect about my friend.**

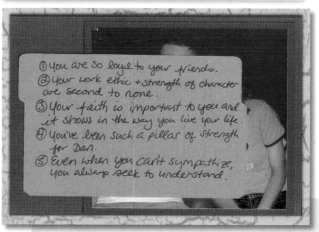

Opening the mini file folder reveals your message for a fun and personal touch.

PAPER CUTS

When journaling by hand, work slowly and turn off the TV! You don't want to be distracted when you're writing—it increases your chances of making a critical error.

Believe it or not, you're nearly done. Now it's time to deal with all those blank panels looming up at you. This is where you're going to write a special letter to your friend. Begin your message on the first blank panel. When you reach the end, simply move to the next blank panel and continue until you've filled up all the blank panels in the album.

You can elect to simply include only your handwriting on these panels. If you want, jazz it up a bit by including chipboard, rub-on, or stickers letters mixed in with your text as I've done in the following figure.

This fun panel contains the end of the letter to the recipient. The addition of rub-on words makes it even more fun to read.

Congratulations! Your accordion is now complete. All that's left is to add some finishing touches.

DECORATING THE COVER

Your accordion comes in a fun folder that just begs to be decorated. Again, this is a quick and easy process.

1. **Adhere your monogram letter to the front of the folder, making sure to place glue on the top flap only.**

2. **Using white rub-on letters, complete the rest of your title.**

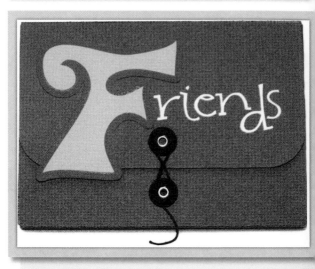

A quick and easy design for your album's folder.

That's it! Place your completed accordion in the embellished folder, and you have a fun and memorable gift for a truly special friend.

PICTURE THIS

Make this gift even more fun and unique by having an entire group of people create it. Gather a group of friends together to honor one person. Have each contributor add a photo and a personal message of his or her own.

CELEBRATING YOUR FRIENDSHIPS

As much as you'd love to, it's probably not practical to create a separate accordion album for every single one of your friends. But that doesn't mean they can't be included in your standard scrapbook albums. Try some of these fun ideas for capturing your friendships in your scrapbook albums.

FRIENDS THROUGH THE YEARS

We all have close friends, those folks we've known for what seems like ages. These are the friends who have shared in so many of our experiences, it's hard to remember what life was like without them. Because your friendship has spanned so many years, sometimes it can be difficult to decide how to document that friendship in a scrapbook.

Try creating a layout based on one of these fun ideas:

- **A "top 10" list of memorable events.**

- **"Our lingo"—create a scrapbook page celebrating those phrases and words unique to your friendship.**

- **Create a page celebrating the reasons you love your best friend. Include silly reasons as well as the serious ones.**

- **Try creating a page with a "what if" theme. If your friend weren't in your life, what would you be missing out on?**

- **Through the years—create a layout featuring a montage of photos and memories from various events, as well as retrospective journaling.**

ORIGINS

Friends can come from all sorts of unexpected places. These days, especially in the world of scrapbooking, many people meet friends online. You might encounter a new friend at your child's school picnic or even waiting in line at the grocery store. Of course, co-workers, classmates, neighbors, and family members often complete our friendship network as well.

Consider creating a layout about how you met one of your friends. Try answering some of the following questions on your scrapbook page:

- **How did you first meet your friend?**

- **Was it an expected friendship?**

- **How long did the relationship take to develop?**

- **How are you alike? How are you different?**

- **What was your first impression of your friend, and how does it differ from the person you know today?**

This fantastic layout showcases a friendship forged in an unexpected place—her daughter's basketball practice sessions.

(Layout by Rachael Giallongo)

This stunning layout features photos from a 16-year friendship. In her journaling, the artist describes what she loves about her friendships and advises her daughters to seek out the same special qualities in their own friends.

(Layout by Tracy Austin)

TIMES TOGETHER

So much of our time with friends is spent just chatting and sharing experiences with one another. Part of the joy of good friendships is that there's much fun to be had simply by being in the same room at the same time, sharing the moment. This time with friends is time well spent. Don't be afraid to bring out your camera and capture the moment.

These fun photos are perfect to feature on a scrapbook page. Complete your page by adding reflective journaling about your friendship or perhaps the moment at hand. Maybe all you have is a photo of the four of you laughing. Do you remember what was so funny? Let the viewers of your page in on the secret.

Do you share any hobbies with special friends? Try creating a layout about time you spend together doing what you love.

This bright layout showcases the artist with some of her favorite scrapbooking friends.

(Layout by Shelley Burkett, Scrapjazz.com design team)

Do you have a favorite "ritual" with a special friend? Perhaps you have a birthday tradition or a particular vacation you enjoy together. Include these photos in your scrapbooks for a record not only of your friendship, but of your favorite activities together as well.

This fun layout features photos from two different years—same place, same theme—for a fun effect.

(Layout by Lorna Palumbo)

ANIMAL FRIENDS

Any pet owner will tell you that many times, her pet is her best friend! Animals show incredible loyalty and are often considered part of the family by their owners. When scrapbooking your friendships, don't forget to create pages celebrating the animals in your life. Include the following details:

- **Your pet's name and the story behind it**
- **The age of your pet**
- **Your pet's pedigree/breeding information**
- **How you came to be the owner of your pet**
- **Your pet's favorite things to do and eat**
- **Fun facts about your pet's personality**
- **What you love most about your pet**

This pretty layout showcases a cat's personality along with a fun memory.

(Layout by Alecia Ackerman Grimm)

THE LEAST YOU NEED TO KNOW

- Accordion albums are fun and easy projects to make. You can often complete one in only a few hours.

- Creating a scrapbook celebrating your love for your best friend is a fantastic gift idea, and the result is keepsake to be cherished.

- When scrapbooking your friend-ships, don't just create pages about events you attended together. Be sure to include details about how you met and why your friendship is important to you.

- Pets are special friends in the lives of those who own them. Making scrapbook pages to honor your pets is a fun way to celebrate that special bond in your albums.

IN THIS PART

This year Grammy and Megan made an Easter cake. We only see Grammy and Papo every few months, so to see them together baking a cake, was so touching. In the short few months that Grammy has been retired, she has taken cake-decorating classes. So not only was she eager to show us the

Part 4

Celebrating Yourself

The idea of creating an entire album (or tour!) all about yourself and the things you love might seem silly to you. But take a minute to look back over the projects you've completed already. Did you take the photos for your vacation album? If so, how many of them were you actually in? What about your child's baby album? Do you show up much there? You're probably beginning to notice a trend. So often, scrapbookers leave an important element out of their creations—themselves.

The idea of creating a scrapbook celebrating your dreams for the future might seem strange now, but imagine what it would be like if you could take a peek into your mother's mind when she was 25. What did she hope for? What was life like on a typical day when your grandmother was raising her family? How was it different from your life today? So often, the answers to these questions are lost. By creating scrapbook albums honoring yourself—your history, the food you love, how you spend a typical week, and the things you dream of—you're creating a true and lasting document of the *real* you. Making these albums is seriously fun. Taking the time to reflect on these things will even help make you a stronger person. And trust me, your grandchildren will thank you.

my life at... twenty five

As my 25th year draws to a close, I sit and wonder whether I could have even planned a better life than the one I have. I've been married to my best friend for four wonderful years and have the sweetest little red-headed much joy to our lives. Our fam...

IN THIS CHAPTER:

- Creating an album celebrating your roles in life, hobbies and interests, favorite things, and more

- Scrapbooking the harder times in your life

- Reflecting on your life so far

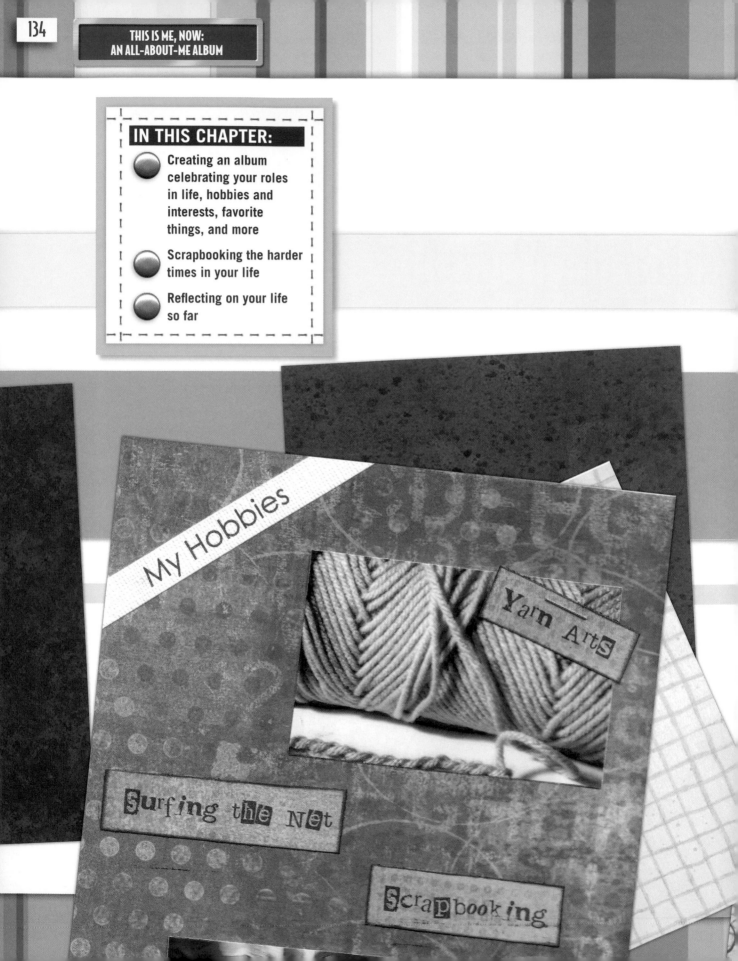

My Hobbies

Yarn Arts

Surfing the Net

Scrapbooking

Chapter **12**

This Is Me, Now: An All-About-Me Album

It's all about you. How often have you thought this (usually accompanied by quite a bit of guilt) only to discover that the world doesn't actually revolve around each of us as individuals? It's truly a mark of becoming an adult when we realize that there's more to life than our own interests. However, that's just not the case with this scrapbook project!

This album *is* all about you—your roles in life, your interests, and more all captured in a handy scrapbook to showcase a true portrait of who you are at this stage in your life. You *are* worth indulging. So kick back, relax, and create this fun project that's just for you.

SCRAP YOURSELF SILLY

Creating this album couldn't be more fun. You finally have a chance to show the world what you're all about as a person! This is a fun and colorful project designed to highlight your personality and interests, all centered around a collection of photographs, words, and phrases.

GETTING STARTED

Begin this project by selecting the aspects of yourself you'd like to feature in your album. Each 2-page spread in this album highlights one set of values, interests, or favorites. There are numerous choices, and this album holds a total of nine sets. (You can always purchase additional page protectors if you'd like to include more.)

Take a moment to think about your life and what defines you. Walk around your home and notice the things you have sitting around: books? plants? a special collection? These are just some of the things you might want to include in your "All-About-Me" album. Consider the following topics as potential categories for your album pages:

• **My roles**	• **My comforts**
• **My history**	• **My worries**
• **My childhood**	• **My fears**
• **My obsessions**	• **My hopes**
• **My rituals**	• **My talents**
• **My beliefs**	• **My weaknesses**
• **My hobbies**	• **My collections**

This is by no means a complete list, so feel free to make up your own topics as well!

A spread about your roles in life offers the viewer a unique perspective into who you are. A few of my roles include fiancée, aunt, artist, and teacher.

After you've selected which topics you'd like to include, take a minute to brainstorm a list of at least 10 things for each of the categories you've selected. If you'd like, jot them down on the worksheet provided in Appendix B to assist you with the album-planning process.

Next, choose three to five items from each list and find a photograph to match. For example, if one of your comforts is scented candles, take a photo of a candle burning in your home. If one of your roles in life is a mother, select a photograph of your children to feature in the album. You'll want to use smaller prints for this album—I highly recommend getting prints made at wallet size to keep the project manageable. Be sure to also print one photograph of you for the title page of your album. Choose something fun that really showcases your personality.

After you've prepared your album text and photographs, you're ready to begin the creation process.

MAKING YOUR ALBUM

Begin by gathering the supplies you'll need to create this album:

- 6×8½-inch Peek-a-View 3-ring binder album (O'Scrap!)
- "Fusion" Patterned Paper Pack (BasicGrey)
- Large script die cut of your first name, white (Headliners by Outrageous Daisy)
- 1 or 2 sheets of white textured cardstock (Bazzill Basics)
- Ribbon (Creative Impressions)
- Black ink pad
- Stapler
- Computer for journaling
- Paper trimmer, adhesive, black pen

This fun album gives the reader a glimpse into what your life is like, as well as what types of things are truly important to you.

The first step in creating your album is to prepare the printed text you'll need. There are two sets of journaling to be printed.

First, print your page titles onto textured white cardstock. I recommend using a 20-point, bold, basic typeface. Simply type out each of your titles into a single word processing document, leaving a few blank lines between each. In addition to each of your titles, be sure to type the phrase *All About*—this will become part of your title page. After your typing is complete, just print, and you're all set. You can easily cut apart the titles later when you're ready to add them to your album pages.

Next, type out the lists of items you chose for each category. Again, typing these onto a single page or two is the easiest way to do it. Try using a fun and funky font for a textured and unique look. After you've typed your list, print it out onto a solid color sheet of patterned paper. (See Chapter 3 if you need help printing on 12×12-inch paper.)

Now that your journaling has been prepared, you can start creating your album's pages. The layout design for this album is quite simple. Each 2-page spread features the title in the upper left corner, with your photos and phrases staggered across the pages.

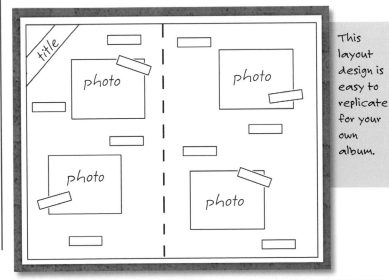

This layout design is easy to replicate for your own album.

Create each spread by following these steps:

1. **Cut a sheet of patterned paper into two 6×8½-inch pieces. These will serve as the base for your layout.**

2. **Cut out the title you want to use, and adhere it diagonally to the upper left corner of your spread. Try placing the title first and cutting the edges to size after adhering it to your layout. This ensures a perfect diagonal cut.**

3. **Add your photographs to the layout.**

4. **Cut out the phrases you selected for this particular layout. Run a black ink pad along each edge of the cut-out word. (This helps the words stand out from the background paper you've selected.)**

5. **Add the phrases that match your photographs to your spread, attaching each on or near its respective photo using a stapler.**

6. **Add the rest of the words and phrases for your category to any remaining space on your layout.**

PICTURE THIS

To make photographed items really stand out, try printing the phrases you use with the photos on paper that is a different color from the rest of the text on your layout.

Repeat these simple steps to create the rest of the layouts for your album. Add each layout to your album as you complete it, and watch as your scrapbook really starts to come together.

FINAL TOUCHES

Now that you've created the bulk of your project, only a few pieces remain.

First, you'll want to create a title page for your scrapbook. Because this project is housed in a semi-translucent binder, remember that this page doubles as your cover.

Creating your title page couldn't be easier. Follow these steps:

1. **Cut a sheet of patterned paper to 6×8½ inches.**

2. **Attach the "All About" title to the upper left corner, as you did for each of your page layouts.**

3. **Add a photo of yourself to the middle of the page.**

4. **Add your die cut name to the bottom of your layout.**

That's all there is to it! When your title page is finished, add it to the front of your album.

This layout has all the pieces in the right place and is a fun tribute to the things I can't live without!

This title page is the perfect start to this album. And the fun photo definitely showcases my personality!

Finally, tie some ribbon through the holes prepunched in the front of your binder. This adds the perfect final touch.

PICTURE THIS

If you'd like, create an "ending" page for this album as well. You could include a list of what you'd like to change about yourself and what you hope will always stay the same. Or try writing a letter to future generations, discussing how you feel about your life right now.

This completed album truly serves as a "time capsule" of your life—who you are today, here and now.

CELEBRATING YOURSELF

Don't have the time to create an entire album all about you? Or maybe you've finished it and want to take the concept a step further. Either way, there are plenty of ways to make beautiful scrapbook pages all about a very special person—you!

THESE ARE THE DAYS

Taking the time to document your life—present and past—for future generations is an important and worthwhile endeavor. These ideas can help you get started creating fantastic pages that document the important pieces of your life:

- Try creating a page showing how your life has changed over a period of time, or showing the events that occurred during that time and reflecting on how they have changed you.

- Spend some time thinking about what your life is like right now. Is it what you imagined for yourself? Record your feelings on a scrapbook page.

- Create a layout highlighting the most significant moments in your life—graduation, marriage, etc. Match them with journaling about how they impacted you. Did the events live up to your expectations? How did you feel when the moment finally arrived?

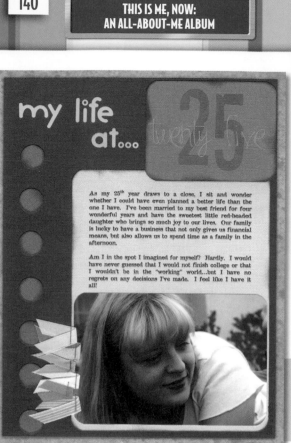

This colorful layout showcases the events of a decade in the life of the artist, along with her feelings about how those years shaped her life and changed her as a person.

(Layout by Rachael Giallongo)

Creating a page showcasing your expectations and feelings about life, such as this simple and classy layout, is a great way to capture the essence of your life on paper.

(Layout by Angie Hagist)

A LITTLE HISTORY, A LOT OF PERSONALITY

Perhaps one of the most fun ways to create scrapbook pages about yourself is to share a little bit of who you are on your pages. Creating a page about your personal and cultural background is a great place to begin. Try making a page centered around one or more of the following ideas:

- **Your ethnicity or race**
- **Your hometown**
- **Your religion**
- **Your career**
- **Your marital status**
- **Your gender**
- **Your roles in life (mother, sister, etc.)**
- **Your personality traits**

There are so many things that make up *you*. Don't leave any out when creating your scrapbooks.

I created this scrapbook page to highlight the many parts of my cultural background and what each of them means to me.

This great layout focuses on many different aspects of the artist's personality.

(Layout by Shaniqua Young)

This layout reveals all sorts of random facts about the artist, from habits and obsessions to wishes for the future.

(Layout by Andrea Steed, co-founder, Scrapjazz.com)

What about your personality? Are you a silly, outgoing person? Perhaps you're shy and introverted. Do you have a secret passion for soap operas? Honor these parts of yourself by creating a special scrapbook page. Try one of these great ideas:

- **Create a "little known facts about me" layout.**

- **Try journaling about the way you show your emotions.**

- **Are you an extrovert or an introvert?**

- **Ask yourself "what if" questions, such as "What if I won the lottery tomorrow?" and record the answers on a layout of your own. (Try the book *If* by Evelyn McFarlane and James Saywell to get a jump-start on this activity.)**

- **Take a personality test online and record the results on a layout.**

Introspection is a rare gift. On this beautiful scrapbook page, the artist reflects on her trusting and open nature.

(Layout by Rachael Giallongo)

SCRAP FACT

Many resources are available to help you with these types of layouts. Try visiting www.tickle.com for a host of IQ tests and personality quizzes, ranging from the professionally developed to the truly bizarre.

SCRAPBOOKING THE HARD TIMES

Unfortunately, life isn't always easy. Many times, unexpected curve balls are thrown our way. We deal with these moments, hopefully grow stronger, and ultimately move on. Although these memories aren't always ones we'd like to remember, they are indeed a part of our lives and should, therefore, be included in our scrapbooks.

I don't necessarily recommend sitting around and dreaming up a list of all the negative things that have happened during your lifetime and creating a scrapbook page about each one, but scrapbooking about difficult times can be an important part of the healing process. If you're in a rough spot right now and need a way to deal with your emotions, or if you've just experienced a personal victory and need to spend some time reflecting on the events that got you there, I do recommend taking the time to create a scrapbook page surrounding the event and your emotions relating to it.

Even if you never show your page to anyone but yourself, the satisfaction you'll get from allowing yourself the freedom to express yourself will be well worth it.

This truly touching and personal page shares the artist's feelings about struggling with her weight during adolescence. It also celebrates her victory in conquering the battle and now living a healthy lifestyle.

(Layout by Tracy Austin)

After my father was diagnosed with cancer, I began wearing a yellow bracelet to show my support for finding a cure. This scrapbook page allowed me to share not only why I wear that yellow band around my wrist, but also explore my feelings about the disease and my appreciation for my dad.

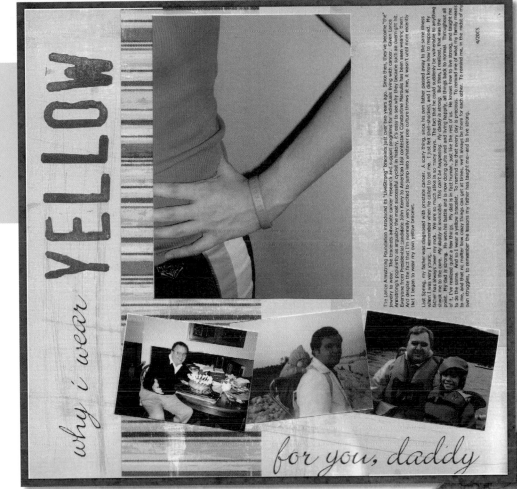

YELLOW

why i wear

for you, daddy

THE LEAST YOU NEED TO KNOW

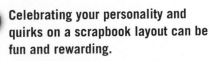 Creating a scrapbook to showcase your personality, interests, and values is a worthwhile endeavor. You'll have fun creating the album, and others will be honored by the chance to see you as you truly are.

Celebrating your personality and quirks on a scrapbook layout can be fun and rewarding.

 Scrapbook pages about events and how they shaped you into the person you are today provide a unique look into yourself.

Taking time to scrapbook the challenges life brings you can be a personally gratifying and healing practice.

IN THIS CHAPTER:

- Creating an album full of your favorite recipes, either to keep or give as a gift

- Telling your family's food stories

- Preserving handwriting from original recipe cards

- Incorporating recipes on traditional scrapbook pages

Isaac's "3-Step Never-Fail" Instructions For

eating blueberries

BLUEBERRY

AUG - 2005

1. squish

2. wave in the sun

3. yum

Chapter 13

Let's Eat: The Recipe Album

Food. Most of us eat at least three times per day. If you add it up, that's quite a bit of time spent in the kitchen! Why is it, then, that something we spend so much time with is given such little significance in our scrapbooks? When you think about it, the food you love says a lot about you. Do you have a weakness for chocolate cake? A certain meal you love to have every year for your birthday? The foods we eat and the traditions surrounding them are truly important to consider and give a lot of insight into our lives.

Where are your favorite recipes stored? Scattered in dozens of cookbooks? Scrawled on the backs of napkins and old index cards? Stuffed in the back of a drawer? Consider creating a special album to showcase your recipe collection and tell the story behind it. It will help you organize your recipes and let you create a beautiful keepsake at the same time. Are your recipes already organized, or are there just too many to count? Try selecting a few of your favorite recipes and making an album for a special friend. It makes an excellent bridal shower or wedding gift, too!

DELICIOUSLY BOUND: CREATING YOUR ALBUM

Creating an album full of your best recipes is a simple project—easy enough to create in a weekend.

GETTING STARTED

As you might have guessed, the first step to preparing for this album is to gather your recipes. At capacity, this album holds 12 recipes in each of 5 categories for a total of 60 recipes. (To help you select your categories and plan your recipes, I've included an Album Planning Worksheet in Appendix B.)

It's easiest to begin by selecting your five recipe categories. Choose ones that mean the most to you and ones you truly love. Some possible categories include the following:

- **Appetizers**
- **Beverages**
- **Soups and Salads**
- **Side Dishes**
- **Entrées/Main Dishes**
- **Beef**
- **Poultry and Fish**
- **Vegetarian**
- **Pasta**
- **Desserts**
- **Cakes and Candy**
- **Cookies**
- **Miscellaneous**

After you've selected your five categories, it's time to choose your recipes. Again, the album can hold a maximum of 12 recipes in each category. After you've gathered your recipes, you'll want to make copies to include in your scrapbook.

The easiest way to copy your recipes is to simply make a quick visit to your local copy store and make a high-quality color copy of each recipe you'd like to include on acid-free paper or cardstock. If you have recipes handwritten onto cards, be sure you check both sides of the card for writing, so each of your recipes is fully included.

PAPER CUTS

Some of your original recipes might need to be reduced to make them fit into this album. Each copied recipe should be no taller than 6 inches and no wider than 7 inches. If your recipes are larger than this, use the copier's reduction feature to get them to size.

If you don't want to use copies of your recipes or don't have high-quality originals to work with, consider typing out your recipes on your computer and printing them out to include them in your scrapbook. Using typed recipes creates a unified look to your album and might be a simpler process for some people. However, note that using copies of handwritten originals provides a truly personal touch to your album. Nana's old cookie recipe might be worth its weight in gold. But Nana's old cookie recipe written out in her own handwriting? That's truly priceless.

I love the look of my grandmother's handwriting on this copy of her original recipe card.

After you've selected your recipes, take a moment to gather some photographs you'd like to include in your album. While you certainly don't need a photo of each recipe you're including, it's a good idea to have a few photos on hand that correspond to the general categories you've chosen to include.

There are a number of directions you can take when selecting your photos. For example, perhaps you've selected "Poultry and Fish" as a category for your album. Because your family goes fishing every year and you love to cook what you catch, you have a number of old family stories and photos relating to your tradition. You could select photos of members of your family fishing or portraits of the people you know who inspired your own love of fishing. Or you might even consider taking a photo of the prepared dish on a plate. Whatever you choose, be sure to gather these photos ahead of time so they're ready when you begin creating your album.

MAKING YOUR SCRAPBOOK

Now that you've gathered your recipes, chosen your categories, and selected a few photographs, it's time to begin creating this fun and beautiful scrapbook. First, be sure you have all the materials you need to get started:

- **8×6-inch ivory spiral scrapbook (Paperbilities by DMD)**
- **12×12-inch Patterned Paper—7 sheets each in 5 patterns, 1 sheet in an additional pattern, and 3 sheets of patterned cardstock (Anna Griffin)**
- **Velvet Alphabet Stickers (Making Memories)**
- **Paper wildflowers (Making Memories)**
- **Small ribbon pieces (Venus Industries, Offray, May Arts)**
- **Ivory colored cardstock**
- **Paper trimmer, adhesive, black pen for journaling**

After decoration, the plain spiral album becomes a gorgeous home to your recipe collection.

To begin your album, open to the first page. Because you're decorating the cover of this album, no introductory page is necessary. You can immediately begin your first category.

In this album, a different patterned paper is used for each category, with a final pattern for the cover. Select the pattern you'd like to use for your first recipe category. Then simply cut your paper into 14 pieces, each measuring 7½ inches wide×6 inches high. (Although this is a 8×6-inch album, the spiral itself takes about ½ inch from the left side of the binding.) Adhere the patterned sheets to the first 14 pages of your album, front and back, completely covering the interior pages.

Next, turn back to the first page. This is your category introduction page. To create this page, follow these simple steps:

1. **Cut a block from your patterned cardstock measuring 7½×2 inches.**
2. **Adhere the cardstock across the lower half of your page.**
3. **Using the letter stickers, place your title on the patterned cardstock.**

This page introduces the cookie section of my album in a fun and colorful way. For an added touch, I used an asterisk sticker to dot the I.

Following the category introduction, include 2 pages that reflect on why you chose the category, what you love about that particular type of food, or that tell a unique story about one or more of the recipes included. This is where you'll want to use those photographs!

You can design these pages any way you like. I elected to first place my photographs on the pages and then add handwritten journaling on ivory cardstock cut into strips that I placed across the length of each page.

Generations of **COOKIE** makers

Grandma, Nana Goff
Mom + Carrie
1974

It seems like all of the best cookie recipes in our family come from the same source - Nana Goff. I don't know if she invented the recipes herself or simply found them in a cookbook. But years later, we're still loving them

Grandma + me
2003

This spread reflects on the women in my family who have loved to bake cookies throughout the past four generations.

Finally, it's time to include the recipes themselves. Placing one recipe per page, simply adhere each recipe to ivory cardstock and then mount it on the center of the page.

This look is all you need for the interior of your album. This particular recipe came to me via e-mail, so I elected simply to type it out.

Ultimate Sugar Cookie & Bakery Icing
Ellen & Becky Meyer

1 1/4 cups sugar	1 cup butter flavored Crisco
2 eggs	1/4 cup light corn syrup
1 Tbsp vanilla	3 cups flour
3/4 tsp baking powder	1/2 tsp baking soda
1/2 tsp salt	

Combine sugar & Crisco. Add eggs, syrup, & vanilla. Add flour, baking power, baking soda, & salt. Roll out & cut with cookie cutters. Bake at 375 degrees on ungreased cookie sheet.

3 1/2 cups powdered sugar	1/2 cup Crisco
2 egg whites (beaten)	1/8 tsp salt
1 tsp vanilla	
optional food coloring	

Cream sugar, Crisco, salt, & vanilla. Add egg whites. Beat until smooth. Tint with coloring if desired. Use decorating bags & tips to frost cookies.

Repeat these easy steps for each category in your album, using a different patterned paper for the background in each recipe category. This not only creates a unified look throughout each section of your album, but also makes it quick and easy to find a particular category while flipping through your album.

DECORATING THE COVER

One of my favorite parts about working with spiral albums is the ability to embellish the entire cover of the album.

Decorating your cover is much like creating each of your category introduction pages. Follow the same basic steps, using the word *Recipes* in place of an individual category title. Be sure you use a strong, dry-based adhesive when attaching the patterned paper to the cover of your album so it won't loosen over time.

Next, adhere a paper flower over the "I" in the word *Recipes*. Because the letter is right in the middle of the word, the flower creates a beautiful addition to your cover.

Finally, cut your ribbon into small pieces, about 2 to 3 inches in length. Tie one piece onto each ring of the spiral using a simple knot. Alternate ribbon designs for an especially fun look.

SCRAP YOUR DINNER

Now that you've created an entire album full of recipes, you're probably wondering about other ways you can include recipes and food in your traditional scrapbook albums. There are tons of fun and exciting ways to do this!

FAVORITE FOODS

Perhaps you're creating an entire large-sized album of your favorite things, or maybe you just want to include a page or two in your albums about the things you really love.

Try one of the following ideas for including a favorite meal or dessert in your traditional scrapbooks:

- **Create a page about your favorite restaurant and the dishes you love to order.**

- **If you could only eat one food for the rest of your life, what would you pick? Why?**

- **Hands down, name your favorite food. Take a photo of it, enlarge it, and create an entire layout about how much you love it.**

- **Have a favorite dish? Include the entire recipe as well as a photo on a scrapbook page.**

Truffles are the centerpiece of this fun layout, which works well as part of an all-about-me album or stands up well on its own.

(Layout by Pam Callaghan)

This fun layout showcases a favorite dessert of the artist, along with a story from her childhood that complements the photograph perfectly.

(Layout by Amy Alvis)

THE TASTES OF CHILDREN

As a child, one of my favorite things to eat was hot dog buns filled with ketchup—only ketchup. As strange as that sounds now, as a preschool teacher—much to my amazement—I discovered that many other young children share this unique love.

Children have very different ways of seeing the world—and food—than adults do. Try capturing this on a scrapbook page in one of the following ways:

- **Include a list of what your child loves—and hates—to eat.**

- **Scrapbook about the *ways* your child likes to eat—her favorite place in the house to have a snack, favorite dinnerware, and more.**

- **Ask your child how to prepare a meal and then write out the "recipe" in his or her own words.**

- **Take a photo of your child cooking with a favorite adult and include it in your album.**

Imagine running into a king-size version of your favorite dessert! That's exactly what happened to this scrapbooker, and she was lucky enough to capture it on film.

(Layout by Rachael Giallongo)

This layout features a child's LEAST favorite foods, which includes everything "spicy." Reflect on your child's unwillingness to eat certain foods in a layout of your own.

(Layout by Julie Ann Stella)

This fun layout dictates the steps of baking a cake through a child's eyes.

(Layout by Rachael Giallongo)

This fun layout shows the unique way in which the artist's child likes to eat blueberries, beginning with step 1: squish the berry.

(Layout by Debbie Hodge)

Cooking with grandparents is a favorite pastime of many children. Consider capturing the moment on a fun scrapbook page.

(Layout by Monica Schoenemann)

THE LEAST YOU NEED TO KNOW

- Creating a recipe album is quick and easy and makes a fantastic keepsake for yourself or to give as a gift.

- Including food and recipes in your traditional scrapbooks is simple and adds a unique twist to your standard scrapbook pages.

- Scrapbooking about food from your child's point of view is humorous and provides fun pages for your albums.

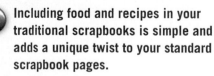

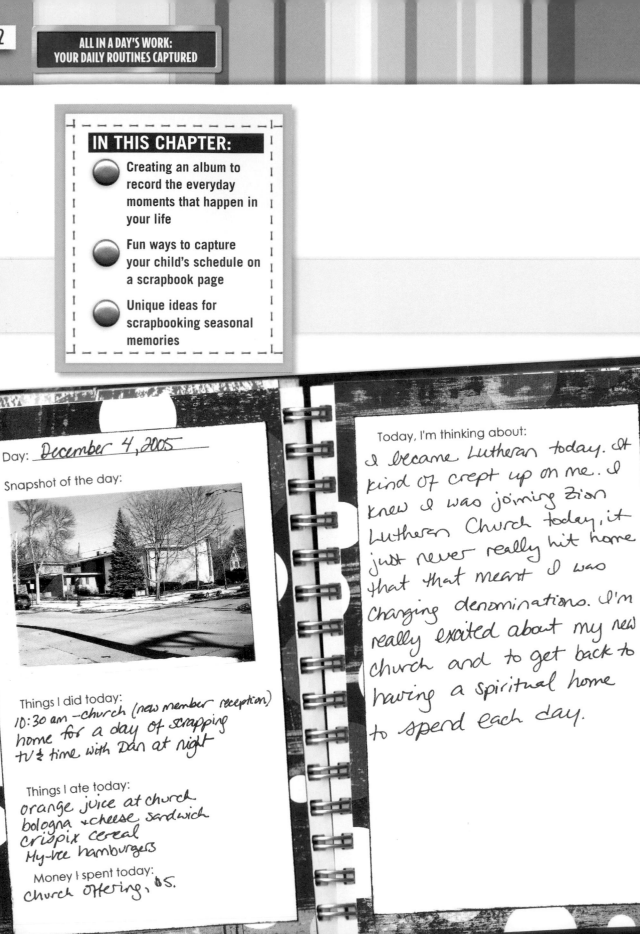

Day: *December 4, 2005*

Snapshot of the day:

Things I did today:
10:30 am – church (new member reception)
home for a day of scrapping
TV & time with Dan at night

Things I ate today:
orange juice at church
bologna & cheese sandwich
crispix cereal
Hy-vee hamburgers

Money I spent today:
church offering, $5.

Today, I'm thinking about:
I became Lutheran today. It kind of crept up on me. I knew I was joining Zion Lutheran Church today, it just never really hit home that that meant I was changing denominations. I'm really excited about my new church and to get back to having a spiritual home to spend each day.

Chapter 14

All in a Day's Work:
Your Daily Routines Captured

Do you ever wonder how your great grandmother spent a typical day? What was life like for her? What did she do with her time? How did she spend her money? If the answers to these questions were readily available, it would provide a true and unique perspective into her daily life. Now think about your own great grandchildren of the future. Do you want them to have the same unanswered questions? To wonder what it was like for you on a typical, ordinary day? To wonder about the things you did, the things you ate, and the things you thought about?

This album project helps you capture the essence of your everyday existence and put it into album form so future generations will indeed know the true you.

CAPTURING THE MOMENT

This album project isn't designed to celebrate significant events in your life. It's not meant to help you recapture your baby's first steps or remember how you spent your first Christmas as a married couple. This project is designed to help you celebrate last Wednesday. Next Saturday. The regular, seemingly insignificant days that make up your life.

CREATING YOUR ALBUM

One of the best parts of this project is that there's no real preparation involved. You don't need to prepare your journaling or print out your photographs. With this project, you get to create the album first and add the details later.

Start by gathering your supplies:

- **8½×5½-inch spiral index tabbed album (Junkitz)**
- **12×12-inch patterned paper—"Salsa" and "Basics" collections (Junkitz)**
- **Button alphabet letters (Junkitz)**
- **Chipboard numbers (Heidi Swapp)**
- **Assorted ribbons (Venus Industries, Creative Impressions, Scrapworks, May Arts)**
- **Black pen**
- **Several sheets of white cardstock**
- **Computer for journaling**

Creating your album is simple and easy. Follow these quick steps to make your own ordinary masterpiece:

1. **For the front and back covers, cut four sheets of brightly colored patterned paper to 8×5¼ inches. Adhere these to the front and back of each cover using a strong, dry adhesive.**

2. **For the first interior page, cut a piece of bright patterned paper to 7¾×4½ inches. Adhere this to the first page.**

3. **Next, cut 24 pieces of neutral-colored patterned paper to 7¾×4½ inches. Adhere these to the interior pages.**

4. **Using a black journaling pen, add numbers to each tab, from 1 to 12, in order.**

PICTURE THIS

Note that this album contains an extra page between each tabbed section. You may use these if you want and create 4 pages for each day you want to feature. I simply chose to remove them.

Now, it's time to print the text for your scrapbook. First, write a short introduction to your album. This should introduce the concept of the album and be short and easy to understand.

Print your introduction on white cardstock. Trim and mount this on a piece of neutral patterned paper, cut to size. Adhere this to the first page in your album.

This fun album serves as the showcase for your collection of ordinary moments.

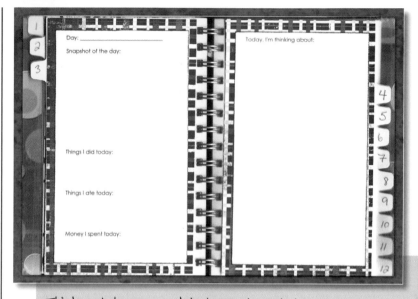

This layout shows a completed spread, ready to go. The edges of the white cardstock were rubbed with black ink to make them stand out.

Next, use your computer to create the basis for your album's interior pages. Decide on three to seven categories of information you'd like to include for each day you choose to record. These will serve as the headings for your journaling later on. Some examples include the following:

- **Things I did today**
- **Places I went today**
- **Things I ate today**
- **Money I spent today**
- **Today, I'm thinking about …**
- **Today, I wish …**
- **People I saw today**
- **Things I learned today**

When you've selected your categories, type them out on your computer, leaving room underneath each heading to write in the required information. Begin each typed entry by leaving a blank line to fill in the date, as well as a "Snapshot of the Day" heading, under which you can add a wallet-size photo.

Print out these blocks on white cardstock, and cut them to 7×4 inches. Adhere them to your album's interior pages.

After you've added your computer journaling headings to your album, take a moment to decorate the album's cover:

1. **Using chipboard numbers, add the number "12" to the top of your cover.**

2. **Follow this with the words *ordinary days* in button letters.**

3. **Finish by tying small ribbon scraps around each spiral. This adds visual interest, as well as hides the plain chipboard visible under the spiral.**

ADDING THE DETAILS

You've done all the work for this album. The cover is beautiful, and the inside is ready to go. All you need to do now is add the details of the days of your life. There are many ways to approach this. You might decide to select a consecutive 12-day period, in which you add to your album every day. You might want to select one day from every month of the year to feature. Or perhaps you'll simply set the album by your bed and add to it as the days go by.

There's no set formula for adding your daily details to your album. Simply pick up a pen and fill in the information for the day you're highlighting. The only addition necessary is a wallet-size photograph from your given day. Many photofinishers can print wallet photographs quite easily, so this shouldn't be very difficult.

PAPER CUTS

As you add to your album, be sure all your photographs are horizontally oriented. Vertical photos are too tall and won't fit in the empty space correctly.

By capturing the everyday moments in your album, you might find that you're revealing parts of yourself that have never before been evident in your albums. Though these days might be ordinary, you'll likely find yourself celebrating them anyway.

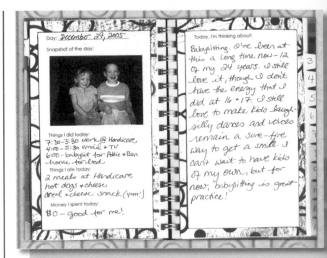

I love this spread. It captures my emotions and love of baby-sitting, something I'd never thought to scrapbook before.

RECORDING THE EVERYDAY

Everyday moments aren't just for this album. By including them in your traditionally-sized scrapbook albums, you'll allow this same "ordinary" part of yourself to shine through.

DAILY ROUTINES

What time do you wake up in the morning? Are you the first one up, or do you wake to the sound of children's feet pattering around your bedroom? These are details worth capturing. Try creating a scrapbook page centered around one of the following topics:

- **Your daily schedule, hour by hour**

- **Are you a morning person or an evening person?**

- **How does your schedule compare to that of your family members?**

- **What is your favorite part of the day?**

- **How do you get to and from work or school?**

- **Where do you spend the bulk of your day? At work? School? Home? In bed?**

- **What are your daily rituals?**

PICTURE THIS

For a unique look, consider using pages from your day planner or calendar directly on a scrapbook layout. Handwriting and all, they provide a glimpse into the real you.

This layout captures every moment of a typical day in the artist's life. Notice how her photographs complement her journaling perfectly.

(Layout by Kim Brown)

A toddler's schedule is much different from anyone else's, as creatively shown here.

(Layout by Linda Harrison)

The emotion and excitement of this young girl's day is perfectly captured in this adorable layout.

(Layout by Becky Lynn Teichmiller)

The emotion and enjoyment of an ordinary day is captured here just beautifully.

(Layout by Michelle Van Etten)

SEASONAL MEMORIES

So often we take the camera outside to capture the changing seasons around us. Beautiful autumn leaves, fun snowy winters, fresh spring flowers, and summer sunshine all find their way into our photo albums. However, sometimes it's hard to know exactly how to include these memories in your scrapbooks. Because they're not often associated with a particular event or theme, placing them can be somewhat difficult.

Why not allow these photographs to take the stage on a layout all their own? Try one of these refreshing scrapbook ideas:

- **Create a layout featuring one photo from each season in a given year.**

- **Take one photo per month in the exact same outdoor location for an entire year and then feature the photos on a layout to show the changing seasons.**

- **Create a page celebrating your favorite season, complete with photographs and a list of why you love it so much.**

PICTURE THIS

Can't seem to get a good seasonal shot of your hometown? Try visiting your city's website or visitor's bureau to find professional photos you can print and use in your scrapbook.

This pretty layout showcases the joy of a changing spring.

(Layout by Tanya-Marie Pocino, owner, Outrageous Daisy)

THE LEAST YOU NEED TO KNOW

- Recording everyday events and ordinary moments in a special album enables future generations to see and know the genuine you, as you really lived.

- Including your daily routine in your scrapbooks can be a fun and worthwhile venture.

- Seasonal memories and photographs, while occasionally difficult to categorize, are a perfect addition to your traditional scrapbook album.

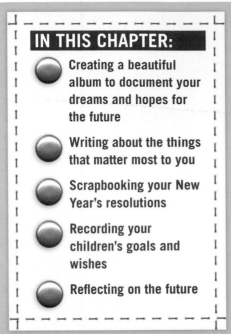
Sing Live,

For years and years, I wanted to be a professional singer. There was no other dream that interested me. While I dabbled in writing when I was younger, and studied it throughout high school and college, I always had music and drama on the brain.

From my first performance in "Oh, Jonah!" – the

One More Time

Slowly but surely, I wasn't singing as much as I once did. But I was scrapbooking. And I was writing. And I was loving it. And so I found that I had changed, and my dreams were no longer what they once were. I now spend my days chasing after new dreams, ones that I find even more rewarding.

But still, there's a part of me that will always want to be up on that stage. The last time I performed was in 2002 with a local band at a bar in Strawberry Point, Iowa. Had I known it would be the last time, it might have been enough.

Chapter **15**

What's Next: Scrapbooking Your Goals and Dreams

Setting goals and making plans is a natural part of life. If you're like me, perhaps your only stumbling block is following through with them! So often, our goals never leave our minds. Or if they do, it's usually only to end up on a piece of scrap paper, later discarded. You can learn a lot about a person by understanding her dreams and goals—what kind of a person she is, and what kind of a person she wants to become.

Think back to when you were a young child. What did you want to be when you grew up? Did you accomplish that? Or do you simply look back and laugh at the person you once were?

Creating a record of your goals and dreams is as much about recording the present as it is about looking to the future. At age 5, I changed my mind nearly every day when it came to deciding my future career. By 17, I was actively pursuing a career in music. Years later, I find myself making a living creating art and teaching others. Perhaps you've been on a steady course for a long time, or maybe you change your mind regularly. Either way, documenting your dreams is a powerful way to showcase your personality and your priorities.

GIVING POWER TO YOUR DREAMS

This classic and beautiful album project helps you put your dreams on paper. Writing down your dreams gives them power and records them for future generations.

As I was creating this project, I included several dreams that had always just been in the back of my mind, things that never really seemed very important. Yet as I began to write down what they meant to me, I discovered a world of possibility that lay right in front of me.

GETTING STARTED

Preparing to create this album is somewhat simple, but it does require quite a bit of introspection. Find a quiet space free from distractions to sit down and reflect. (Turn to Appendix B for a worksheet to help you with this process.)

First, create a list of dreams and wishes for your future. It doesn't matter if some of them seem silly or outlandish—they are your dreams, and this is your own personal record. The most important thing is to be honest with yourself.

If you get stuck, try pondering the following questions:

- **If I could have any career without regard to money, geographic location, or any other hindrance, what would it be?**

- **If I could spend an entire week doing just one thing for fun, what would I choose?**

- **How is my family currently structured? Do I want this to change (i.e., get married, have a child, etc.)?**

- **Are any dreams left over from my childhood that I don't want to part with?**

- **Is there any place on Earth I'm truly longing to go, for a vacation or otherwise?**

- **Are there any people or groups I want to meet or join?**

- **How do I feel about the person I am today? Are there any things I don't like about myself? What do I want to change?**

Aim for at least 8 goals, and probably no more than 20. The sky is indeed the limit, but you don't want to overextend yourself or your album!

After you've created your list of goals and written them down, select two photos from your collection to accompany each goal. It's easier than you might think to gather photos to represent your feelings about events that haven't yet happened. For example, on my layout about wanting to visit all 50 states, I included favorite photos from 2 of the states I have visited—Wyoming and Alaska.

This layout about wanting to see the entire nation consists of fun photos as well as reflections on the goal, including where I've already been and the remaining states I most look forward to visiting.

After you've gathered your dreams, photos, and thoughts, you're ready to begin.

Visit all

Despite my avoidance to all things "out of the routine," there is a deep-rooted part of me that loves all things beautiful. I want to see this entire Nation, and all that it has to offer. I grew up in a family that travels, and still desire to be a traveler at heart. So far, I've been to 26 out of the 50 states.

The ones I loved the most are Alaska, Wyoming, and North Carolina. And though I'm quickly becoming an Iowa girl at heart, Maryland still holds the distinction of being my favorite place I've ever held residence in.

50 States

There's a lot of country left to see. I've never really been exposed to the Pacific Northwest or the Deep South, so perhaps those are the areas most intriguing to me. Hawaii holds its charms as well—it will be hard to resist those beautiful oceans.

CREATING THE ALBUM

To make this stunning album, you'll need the following:

- 6×12-inch "Book Look" Scrapbook Album (Karen Foster Design)
- 11 to 20 sheets of "Diamond Antiquity" patterned paper (Karen Foster Design)
- Violet photo corners (Chatterbox)
- 1 yard decorative ribbon (Venus Industries)
- "Dream" metal charm (Karen Foster Design)
- Computer for journaling
- Paper trimmer, adhesive

This classic album is the perfect choice to hold your collection of dreams and wishes. Its timeless look provides you with an album you'll cherish for years to come.

PAPER CUTS

The amount of supplies you need for this album greatly depends on the number of goals you're including. This album holds enough pages for eight dreams, plus your title, introductory, and conclusion pages. If you want to include additional goals, be sure to pick up an extra pack of refill pages, as well as some additional patterned paper when you purchase your album.

The page layout for this album is quite simple. The album is designed to hold 6×12-inch pages, so each two-page spread for this album is a perfect 12×12 inches.

Most of the work of creating this album happens at your computer. Laying out your pages is quick and easy:

1. Start by opening your word processing program.

2. Enter the page setup option. Set your paper size to legal, with the following margins: top (.5 inches), bottom (2.5 inches), left (1.25 inches), right (2.75 inches).

3. Type in your page text. Keep each side of your spread on a separate page. Put half of your title at the top and then add your journaling. Include your thoughts from your time spent reflecting. Be sure to say why achieving the goal is important to you. Leave room between paragraphs to mount a photograph after printing. Repeat this process on the second page to create the other half of your two-page layout.

Follow this simple page layout to create a timeless and elegant look.

Title   Title

photo

photo

4. Cut each sheet of 12×12-inch paper in half to fit your album. Print your text, one page at a time, on your patterned paper. (See Chapter 3 if you need assistance with printing on odd-size sheets of patterned paper.)

5. After printing your text, mount your photographs on your pages using photo corners.

PAPER CUTS

The margins and paper sizes given here work well, but keep in mind that all word processing programs and printers work a bit differently. It's a good idea to run a test page through your printer first to check the alignment of your text against your patterned paper, and also to be sure you've allowed enough room to include your photographs. If you're still having trouble, consider creating standard journaling blocks and adhering them to your page, instead of printing directly on the patterned sheet.

Follow these simple steps to create a two-page spread for each of your specially chosen goals.

This spread comes together quite nicely ... my thoughts on having a child someday, matched with a photo from my days teaching preschool, as well as one of my own baby pictures.

FINAL TOUCHES

As with most albums, your project isn't truly complete until you've added a title page and a conclusion. You might want to add an introductory page spread as well.

When creating a title page for this album, less truly is more. Follow the same basic layout from your album pages. Include a title for your album, your name, and the date or your age.

PICTURE THIS

Because the patterned paper for this album design features a border, cut your title page out of the middle of a 12×12-inch sheet instead of just using one side. You'll have an elegant and balanced border running across the top and bottom of your page.

This title page has all the necessary elements to create the perfect look.

It's difficult to include larger amounts of introduction or reflection on a title page alone, so you might want to follow your title page with an introductory spread. This is a great place to share your thoughts on the nature of your goals and why you chose to record them. Create this page as you're completing your album. Having already gone through the process of writing out your dreams, you'll have new insights to share and include.

Dreamer *By Nature*

This introductory page explores feelings about following dreams, the status of "dreams in progress," and reflections on the future.

Finally, as with most albums, it's a great idea to include one final page to close your album. Because this album is all about works in progress, there's no one right way to end your album. Try one of the following ideas to finish your album with flair:

- **Include a checklist of all your dreams, with room to write in the dates as they come true.**

- **Make a prediction about which of the dreams you think you can truly attain and which ones will be harder for you.**

- **Include an inspirational photo and quote.**

- **Have a friend or family member (or several!) write an encouraging message to help keep you motivated to follow your dreams.**

EMBELLISHING YOUR ALBUM COVER

This album is already quite stunning, but adding a decorative touch goes a long way.

1. **Take a length of ribbon and tie it around the outside of the album, finishing with a large bow on the outside of your album.**

2. **Attach the "Dream" metal charm to the bow on your album. The charm features a hole to make threading it onto ribbon quick and easy; however, if you're using particularly wide or thick ribbon, you might find it easier to attach the charm using a hot glue gun or industrial-strength adhesive.**

This charm adds the perfect touch to this album cover and gives just the tiniest hint about what is found inside.

SCRAP FACT

Charms aren't just for bracelets anymore! Check your local craft store for charms in all kinds of shapes and sizes. You're bound to find the perfect fit for any project.

CELEBRATING THE FUTURE

Perhaps you're just not ready to write down all your dreams. Or maybe you did and want to find other ways to include more of your feelings and reflections in your traditional scrapbooks. Whether you want to record your resolutions for the new year, write down next week's "to-do" list, or reflect on the future of your child, you can scrapbook the future in plenty of ways before it arrives.

RESOLUTIONS AND WISHES

Once every year, a vast majority of the world sits down and writes out their goals for the coming year. Diets are started. Diaries are commenced. Plans are written. For so many people, though, the effect begins to wear off rather quickly. By February, most New Year's resolutions have already been forgotten—at least until next year, when they'll be pulled out once more.

Creating a scrapbook page to record your resolutions is one way to ensure they aren't forgotten. Taking the time to showcase your list creatively makes you spend more time thinking about them and gives you a stronger desire to follow through.

PICTURE THIS

For added motivation, try framing your resolutions scrap-book page and displaying it prominently. You'll have a constant reminder of where you want to be headed for the coming year.

Sometimes, our goals aren't shaped by a desire for self-improvement or even necessarily a deep-rooted desire. Are there random things you hope for? Perhaps you've always wanted a pet but could never have one. Maybe there's a special item you've always wanted to buy. Dreaming of owning a vintage car? All these things are scrapbook-worthy.

Look online for photos to accompany these fun pages, or try searching through magazines or books for the perfect accent.

This colorful layout does a wonderful job of displaying the artist's goals for the coming year. Notice how the journaling is kept in pockets. It serves as a reminder for the artist, while also maintaining a little bit of privacy.

(Layout by Alison Lidell)

A scrapbook page featuring the dogs I've always wanted. Maybe someday!

(Animal photography by Cheryl K. Kardas, Patricia Marroquin, and Tina Rencelj)

THE DREAMS OF CHILDREN

Children are far more in touch with their dreams than adults are. Just ask any child about what she wants her grown-up life to be like, and you'll likely get quite an earful. The dreams of children are just as scrap-worthy as our own. Record these dreams on pages for their scrapbooks. Trust me, they'll thank you for it.

Does your child dream of becoming a world-famous artist? A firefighter? A classical musician? A businessman? The dreams of children change all the time. One of the most important things adults can do for them is to let them know that it's okay to be a dreamer and that their dreams will be supported and encouraged.

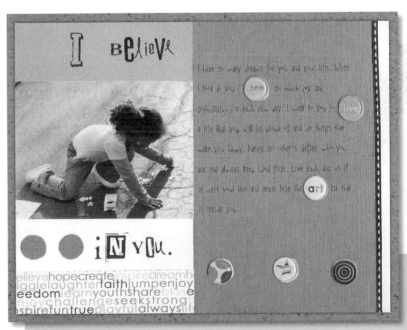

In the form of a message to her daughter, this artist showcases her own hopes and dreams for her child.

(Layout by Marie Cox)

While eating dinner one night, you decided to share with us what you wanted to do when you got older*. When we realized this was not going to be a short list, Daddy got a paper and pencil to jot everything down.

Things you will eat:
- salad
- hamburgers
- onions
- olives
- lettuce
- carrots
- sausage

Things you will do:
- drive a car
- play soccer
- go to the purse store
- ride a horse
- ride a cow
- put on a ring
- vacuum
- watch commercials**
- play music
- shoot guns
- be a dentist

Things you want Katie to be:
- a doctor
- a ballerina
- a pumpkin

*10 years of age
**everything but cartoons

when I get
older

DEC 2004

This hilarious layout captures the dreams of a child in her own words. Becoming a dentist, riding a cow, and eating onions are just a few of the things this young girl plans to do with her life.

(Layout by Moon Ko)

Consider capturing your child's heroes and role models on a scrapbook page. Whether your child is in love with a certain cartoon character, idolizes the boy down the street, or simply—as so many children do—looks up to his or her parents, reflecting on the individuals who influence your child can be the perfect basis for a truly unique scrapbook page.

APR 29 2005

This child is already—quite literally—following in his father's footsteps.

(Layout by Shaniqua Young)

LOOKING AHEAD

Sometimes, it's impossible to know where the future will take you. Perhaps you're just beginning a new relationship or phase of your life. Maybe you're pondering a move or career change. Journaling can often be a helpful and healing tool when dealing with the emotions that come with major—and minor—life changes.

Consider creating a scrapbook page reflecting on the future that lies ahead of you. Need some pointers? Try one of the following prompts to help you get started:

- **What will my life be like one year from now? Five years? Ten?**

- **How will my life change after I get married? Have a child? Become a grandparent?**

- **What will life bring after completing school or specialty training?**

- **What changes do I anticipate after changing where I live?**

- **How will I feel after I achieve a certain goal?**

Reflecting on the changes life might bring can help you prepare for them. Including them in your scrapbooks helps preserve a snapshot of your life as you truly live it.

Including a lot of journaling on your pages is a great way to capture your feelings. This simple and pretty design matches the artist's words perfectly.

(Layout by Julie Norton)

THE LEAST YOU NEED TO KNOW

 Creating a scrapbook full of your dreams for the future is a powerful way to document your personality and priorities, as well as give you motivation to chase down your goals.

 Recording your New Year's resolutions on a scrapbook page is a fun and effective way to plan your resolutions and help you work toward achieving them.

Spending time reflecting on your dreams for the future can be a powerful and worthwhile experience.

 Documenting your children's dreams and heroes is a fabulous way to capture their spirit and enthusiasm.

Using your scrapbooks as a place to journal your feelings about the future can be a powerful experience.

Part 5

Sharing the Love

Now that you're a seasoned scrapbooker, it's time to share your hobby with others. Start by creating a fun and easy album with a special young girl in your life. This project allows you to work with her to learn to express her creativity plus create an album she'll treasure long into her adult years. Next, create a scrapbook with a group of friends centered around a specific theme. Your friendship will grow along with your artistic skill—plus, you'll have a beautiful album brimming with art from several different people—a truly unique scrapbook. Finally, take a step out of the album by creating cards, wall décor, and even refrigerator magnets to share with people close to you.

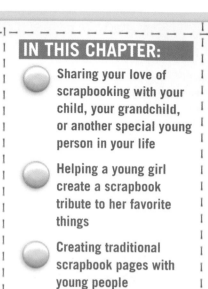

IN THIS CHAPTER:

- Sharing your love of scrapbooking with your child, your grandchild, or another special young person in your life

- Helping a young girl create a scrapbook tribute to her favorite things

- Creating traditional scrapbook pages with young people

- Commemorating the experience of shared scrapbooking in your own scrapbooks

Cookies

FAMILY

Chapter **16**

Her Favorite Things: Sharing Your Hobby

Many of the best things in life are meant to be shared, and the joy of scrapbooking is no exception. If you're anything like me, you decided to start scrapbooking to preserve a few photographs in a nice album. Now you're hooked, and it's time to share the enthusiasm you've acquired as well as the knowledge you've obtained.

Scrapbooking with other adult friends is an incredibly fun activity and offers rewards for everyone involved. (For a fun project to do with a group of women, turn to the next chapter.) Sharing your hobby with a younger person, however, can be thrilling and satisfying in its own unique way. Take a moment to think back to when you were just 12 or 13 years old. What were you passionate about? What types of things did you love? Who did you look up to? Now imagine if you had a visual record of all those things. Taking the time to scrapbook with a young adult in your life—and give her the opportunity to create an album celebrating the things she loves—is the perfect way to show you care.

SCRAPPING WITH TEENS AND PRETEENS

Okay, so maybe right now you're starting to think that I'm just a little bit crazy. The idea of allowing a teen to enter your home, your kitchen, and (*gasp!*) your scrapbook space can seem a little daunting at first—especially if you're not a parent. But trust me, scrapping with a younger person truly *is* a rewarding experience.

Sharing your knowledge of this fun hobby can be quite meaningful. You'll likely gain confidence in your ability as a scrapbook artist as well as pick up a few tips and tricks along the way. Young people see the world through different eyes—their approach to scrapbooking might be completely different from anything else you've tried. And you just might love it.

PICTURE THIS

Not only is scrapbooking with teens fun, but it's also a great way to use up your extra supplies! Your leftover stickers and die cuts are a treasure for these young artists.

If you're a parent or grandparent of a young girl age 10 to 14 or so, this project is obviously for you. But if you're not, don't skip over this project entirely without reading on.

There are plenty of ways to get involved with young people, even if you don't have children of your own. Maybe a friend of yours has a child you'd like to work with. Consider getting involved with a local Big Brothers Big Sisters program or 4-H club. Your community likely offers plenty of ways for you to connect with young people in your area. Whether you choose to work on this project with a child of your own, or a group of children you've just met, chances are you won't regret it.

For this project, I turned to a pair of girls I've known for several years. I met Jenny and Ashley when I volunteered as a helper for a local Girl Scout troop during my years as a college student. They were in first grade at the time. Now, as new junior high school students, Jenny and Ashley were very excited about the prospect of creating something uniquely them—often a difficult thing to do in the tumultuous junior high years.

PICTURE THIS

This project and the examples shown are designed with young girls in mind, but don't be afraid to share your love of scrapbooking with your son or another special young man. Simply adapt the papers and products you use to create a fun and masculine album.

GETTING READY

One of the most important things to do when approaching this project is to first determine the level of scrapbooking experience your young artist possesses. If she's new to the hobby, take some time to share with her the things you learned in the first part of this book. A few quick lessons are all that's really necessary. You'll want to be sure she has a basic understanding of how to assemble the parts of a scrapbook page, as well as the skills necessary to use simple scrapbooking tools.

Next, explain the album concept. This is a fun scrapbook for young people to create. The album consists of a title page, followed by a page devoted to each of their favorite things. Start by having your young scrapper make a list of the things she loves most. Every girl's list is going to be different, and there are bound to be at least a few things that surprise you. Following is a sampling of Ashley and Jenny's favorite things:

- **Family members: siblings, uncles, cousins, and parents**
- **Pets**
- **Cookies**
- **Scrapbooking and other crafts**
- **Sports**
- **Makeup**
- **Books, movies, music, and video games**
- **Holidays**
- **Vacation spots**

When your girl's list is complete, have her find or take a photo to represent each item on her list. She should select one additional photo of herself for the cover page as well. Be sure you have prints of all the chosen photos, and you're ready to begin.

PAPER CUTS

Be sure you use copies of your original photos for this project, especially if you're using family photographs. Remember that these photographs won't end up in your own albums.

GATHERING MATERIALS

Selecting the products for this album is one of the best parts of the process. It's important to remember that because it's not your album, you shouldn't be the one choosing the products. Depending on your budget and relationship, consider taking a trip to a local scrapbook store together and letting her select her own products. If that's not possible, choose a few items from your own stash of supplies, and allow her to select from them.

These albums show the unique personalities of their creators.

(Albums by Ashley Orr and Jenny Barnes)

The items you'll need for this project include the following:

- **6×6-inch album with page protectors**
- **Coordinating patterned paper or cardstock**
- **Lettering tools (Rubber stamps, die-cut letters, and a simple black pen are all excellent choices.)**
- **Stickers or accents to match the photos selected (optional)**
- **Embellishments for the album's cover, if applicable**

To start the project, I chose to give Jenny and Ashley each a 6×6-inch album from SEI's preservation series. The album's slim and unique design allowed each girl to customize the album to make it her own. Plus, at only $4.99 each, they were the perfect choice for a project of this nature.

Beyond that, each girl made her own decisions. Jenny opted for a purple-and-blue patterned paper collection (Coastline by Making Memories) and to use die-cut letters (Wet Paint by Sizzix) to create the majority of her titles. She also used a few rubber stamps and hand lettering in her album. Ashley elected for a pink-and-orange paper combination (also Coastline by Making Memories) and chose to use a mix of rubber stamps (Image Tree by EK Success), die-cut letters (Girls are Weird by Sizzix), and her own handwriting to create the page titles in her album. Both girls also decided to use a selection of ribbon, paper flowers, and rhinestones to add the finishing touches to their albums.

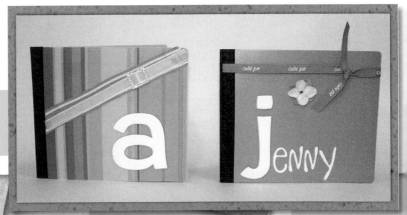

CREATING THE ALBUM

The goal of this project is to allow each young scrapbook artist to create her own scrapbook, in her own style. For this reason, the process of actually creating the album is very simple.

To begin, the artist should select a single photo of herself and mount it on a piece of 6x6-inch paper. Then, using any technique, add the title "My Favorite Things."

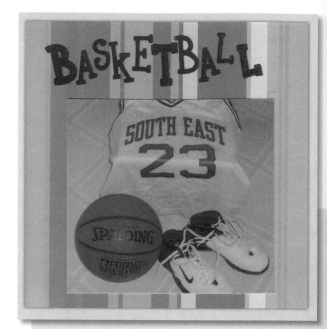

This simple page with die-cut lettering is perfect for displaying Ashley's love of playing basketball.

(Layout by Ashley Orr)

These title pages feature fun photographs and simple titles.

(Layouts by Jenny Barnes and Ashley Orr)

Next, your artist should create a single page layout for each of her favorite things. The layout design for these pages is quite simple and should be open to interpretation by the artist.

When she gets into the work of creating the pages, she'll likely want to change the design occasionally to accommodate what's being featured. Encourage this! This album is an exercise in creativity, and you don't want the artist to feel stifled by a design scheme or feeling of what the album "should" look like.

This pair of sketches shows just a couple ways the page designs can be laid out.

The military-themed stickers on this spread are an ideal match for these photographs of Jenny's brother, currently enlisted in the U.S. Army.

(Layout by Jenny Barnes)

The addition of rhinestones and a hand-drawn design was the perfect choice for this layout.

(Layout by Ashley Orr)

Encourage your artist to add each page to her album as she completes it. The pages in this album can be included in any order.

FINAL TOUCHES

After all the album's pages are complete, the artist might want to decorate the cover of the album she's selected. Again, there's no right or wrong way to do this. Encourage her to select embellishments or papers that suit her personality and match the basic color and design scheme she selected for her album.

Finally, ask her to sign and date her album. A great place for this is the front or back inside cover of the album. In years to come, she'll enjoy seeing her signature as it once was. (Note: this idea was actually suggested to me by Ashley herself. Don't forget that you can learn a lot by scrapping with a younger artist!)

Her special album is now complete, and you've helped her create a book she'll treasure for a lifetime.

PICTURE THIS

This album project isn't just for teens. Try making a small album of your own favorite things through the years.

EXPANDING ON THE EXPERIENCE

Now that you've had the pleasure of scrapbooking with a young woman, consider the different ways to expand on the experience. Perhaps you'll want to encourage your artist to create a traditional scrapbook of her own. If nothing else, take the time to create a page for your own larger album documenting the experience and how it made you feel.

FAVORITE THINGS, ONE STEP FURTHER

Although the young artist you love has already completed her album of favorite things, it's quite likely that she's now developed the same love of scrapbooking you have. Chances are, she's just getting started in the hobby and now wants to complete even more projects.

Many of the album projects in this book are suitable for young scrapbookers. In particular, the school memories album (Chapter 7), friendship album (Chapter 11), and goals album (Chapter 15) are good projects for younger adults. You might find that your young scrapbook artist would simply like to create a large traditional scrapbook of her own, adding pages from events and moments that inspire her.

Taking the leap from small, themed scrapbook to large, complex scrapbook might be a daunting task for a young artist. Keep the process simple by encouraging her to start with what's already familiar.

This finished page shows some of Jenny's favorite photos of her dog, along with descriptive journaling. Jenny designed this layout completely on her own.

(Layout by Jenny Barnes)

This page about Jenny's dog was perfect for her favorite things album.

(Layout by Jenny Barnes)

After creating a page about her dog as part of her album project, Jenny discovered that she still had quite a few photos of her dog that she wanted to include in her scrapbook art. Jenny already owned a 12×12-inch scrapbook, so she decided to create a large page about her dog she could add to her album.

Again, I left product selection up to the artist. Jenny chose a fun animal-print paper, along with coordinating cardstock, twill, and a metal charm by Flair Designs.

RECORDING YOUR EXPERIENCE

By now, you probably have some great memories of your scrapbooking experience with younger people. These memories are scrapbook-worthy on their own. Take some time to create a scrapbook page or two for your traditional scrapbook, commemorating your experience.

Consider any of the following approaches when creating your pages:

- **Include photos of your young scrapbook artist doing what she loves, or a photo of the two of you together.**

- **Create a "top 10" list of the things you learned while scrapbooking together.**

- **Reflect on your relationship with the young scrapper.**

- **Compare and contrast your similarities and differences, both as individuals and in your approaches to scrapbooking.**

- **Journal about what your own favorite things were as a young person and how times have changed from then to now.**

This layout captures the fun I have when scrapbooking with Ashley. The mini file folder flips up to reveal hidden journaling reflecting on our experience.

THE LEAST YOU NEED TO KNOW

- Scrapbooking is a hobby that's meant to be shared, regardless of the age of the artists.

- Scrapbooking with a young adult is a worthwhile and rewarding experience.

- Creating an album celebrating favorite things is a fantastic first project for any young person.

- Take time to document your shared experience on a scrapbook page just for yourself.

IN THIS CHAPTER:

- Creating a collaborative album with a group of friends or acquaintances

- Choosing a theme and assembling your album

- Dealing with conflict in the circle, should it arise

- Looking at a sampling of circle journals

Chapter **17**

A Collaborative Scrapbook:
The Circle Journal

So far, you've created several scrapbook projects for others. And you even helped someone else create a scrapbook for herself. Now it's time to take the act of scrapbooking with others to the ultimate end and create a collaborative scrapbook, or a circle journal.

CIRCLE JOURNALS: A BRIEF HISTORY AND INTRODUCTION

The idea of creating art collaboratively is hardly a new idea. The origins of the *circle journal* phenomenon can be traced to the quilting bees of the 1800s, in which a group of women got together to create a quilt for a special person or occasion. Each woman contributed a square to the finished quilt.

SCRAP SPEAK

A **circle journal** is a scrapbook album that's created by an entire group of individuals. Circle journals are often unified by a central theme or subject to which all artists respond.

The modern circle journal isn't all that different from its quilted predecessor. To create a circle journal, the first step is to find a group of women with whom to collaborate. Each artist then decides on a theme or concept of her own choosing and creates an album based around that theme. After she's created her own entry, she passes it to the next person in the circle and also receives a journal from another woman in the group. She then creates a journal in her friend's album, according to the theme of that particular album. Each journal travels around the circle to each artist before heading home to its original owner.

To share the joy of circle journals with you, I enlisted the help of six extraordinarily talented women:

- **Alecia Ackerman Grimm**, whose eclectic style you're surely familiar with. Alecia's work has appeared in nearly every major industry magazine, including *Creating Keepsakes, Simple Scrapbooks, Scrapbook Trends, Memory Makers,* and *Scrapbooks Etc.*—just to name a few. Alecia's pages are always full of color and detail and are a joy to experience.

- **Leah Blanco Williams**, a freelance writer and design artist for *Memory Makers* magazine as well as a *Creating Keepsakes Hall of Fame* honorable mention winner. Leah's artistic and unique style truly makes her work stand out in a crowd.

- **Rachael Giallongo**, who is no stranger to the world of circle journals. Rachael was a primary contributor to the book *Circle Journals* published by Pinecone Press in mid-2005 and is the co-author of *The Office Book,* also from Pinecone Press. Rachael's designs are always strong, and her voice is always sincere.

- **Angie Hagist**, whose clean-line style you'll probably recognize from the pages of *Simple Scrapbooks* and *CorrespondenceART* magazines. Angie's ability to produce beautiful art in a simple style is second to none.

- **Alexis Hardy**, the design team coordinator for The Scrapbook Stand, is also a nationally published artist. Alexis' beautiful handwriting adorns nearly every page she designs, and the messages she writes are always heartfelt—she is a true original.

- **Michelle Van Etten**, an artistic scrapbooker with a flair for the truly dramatic. An up-and-comer in the world of scrapbooking, Michelle currently serves on the design teams of Outrageous Daisy, Prima, and Spellbinders. Michelle's extravagant pages are true works of art.

Together, the seven of us embarked upon our own circle journal journey. Want to participate in a circle of your own? Read on.

FINDING AND JOINING A CIRCLE

The first step in participating in a circle journal project is to find a group of 6 to 12 interested artists. If you have a group of friends in your hometown who are all active scrapbookers, you've got it made. If not, there are still many ways to connect with other women and create a circle journal. If you'd like to form a group within your community, try one of these options:

- **Call your local scrapbook store and ask if they would be interested in hosting a circle journal for customers.**

- **Check into local artists groups or other groups where you might find women who would be interested in creating a collaborative album.**

- **Post a flyer at a local hobby or craft store inviting those interested to contact you.**

If you're willing to make a few trips to the post office for your journal, there are many more options available to you. Many online scrapbooking sites have message boards and forums where you can post your interest in a circle journal, and groups frequently form from these boards. Participating in a journal project with artists from around the country can be an exhilarating experience and generally results in a beautiful finished album.

PAPER CUTS

Unfortunately, not everyone you meet online is trustworthy. If you're planning a circle journal project with a group of women online, be sure you have accurate contact information, including a phone number, for everyone in your group.

When you've gathered a group of friends together, or found them online, you'll need to take some time to work out some details and set up the logistics for the group.

CHOOSING A HOSTESS AND SETTING GROUND RULES

Every circle journal group should have a hostess. This person sets the rules for the group, makes sure everyone honors her commitments, and handles any conflicts, if they should arise. In general, the hostess is usually the one who initiates the idea of starting the circle journal group. If possible, the hostess should be someone who has participated in at least one circle journal project before.

After the hostess is selected, the group needs to decide on the ground rules for the circle. Things that need to be discussed include the following:

- **How long each participant should keep each journal. Two weeks to one month is the perfect amount of time. Often the group decides on a specific date (e.g., the first of each month) to trade their journals.**

- **Method of distribution. If you're going to be sending circle journals through the mail, you'll want to agree on mailing guidelines including how each journal should be packed and whether or not insurance should be purchased.**

- **Ways to keep in touch. For long-distance and Internet-based groups, I believe the best way to do this is to set up an e-mail distribution list using the Groups feature at Yahoo.com. Participants can send notices to the group whenever they mail or receive a circle journal from another participant. Yahoo Groups also offers image galleries so participants can share their work with each other, as well as database functions so participants can keep each other's contact information handy.**

- **Theme and size of albums. Most circle journal groups do not create specific rules about this, and each artist is allowed to choose her own theme and album. In some circles, the hostess** must approve the themes so no two participants have the same theme. Sometimes, especially if journals are going to be mailed, the hostess might want to put a size restriction on albums to maintain ease of mailing; anything larger than 9×9 inches is often considered too large.

After you've set up all the ground rules for your group, the fun can begin—it's time to start creating your album.

PLANNING YOUR CIRCLE JOURNAL

Before you do anything else, you need to decide on the theme of your album. This can be anything from "Favorite Foods" to "Family Traditions." The themes we chose for our circle included the following (the originator of each album is listed in parenthesis):

- **Beauty (Allyson)**
- **Hometowns (Angie)**
- **Favorite Photographs (Michelle)**
- **One Day—Predictions for the Future (Leah)**
- **Serendipity—Happy Accidents (Alexis)**
- **My Five Senses (Rachael)**
- **Gal Pals (Alecia)**

Feel free to use any of these themes for your circle journal project. Additional ideas include the following:

- **Favorite Things**
- **I Believe**
- **Art**
- **Pet Peeves**
- **Music and Entertainment**
- **Vacations**
- **Daily Rituals**
- **Careers**
- **I Wish**

When you've selected a theme, you can begin the process of creating your album.

PICTURE THIS

For even more circle journal ideas, try searching online. The best way to choose the topic for your journal is to think about something you love or that's important to you. It should be something you're excited to share with others, but also something you want others to share with you.

CREATING A CIRCLE JOURNAL

The first step in creating your circle journal is to select the products and album you'd like to use. Generally, it's a fun idea to pick products and colors that complement the theme you've chosen. You'll want to be sure you have enough products to make several introductory pages.

For the introductory pages in my circle journal on beauty, I chose to combine these gorgeous pastel papers by 7gypsies with chipboard images of vintage beauty queens.

There are several parts to each circle journal, which should be created in order.

First, you'll need to create a title page for your album. This should include the album's theme as well as your name, if you like.

Angie's title page clearly showed her album's theme and also reflected her fun scrapbook style.

After you've created a title page, you should create an introductory page. This page introduces the artist to your theme and invites them to participate. It also enables you to make any specific requests you might have for your album. For example, Angie requested that each artist create an entry about the town in which they currently reside, even if it doesn't always feel like their true hometown.

Alexis perfectly describes the theme of her circle journal and lets each artist know exactly what type of entry to create in her album.

Following the introductory page comes the sign-in page. This is a page or spread on which each artist is instructed to leave her own personal mark. Every album is different, so it's important to read the directions to know how to proceed.

Michelle's sign-in page included blank tags for each participant to decorate with their name and photograph.

Leah's album required each artist to add a photo of herself, as well as sign in on a library card.

There are many unique ways to create a sign-in page for your album. Try a pocket page full of tags or a library card in a pocket for each artist to sign. In addition to signing in on the designated page, Leah had each of us place our thumbprint in her album using an ink pad. For a "Favorite Books" themed circle journal, I once asked participants to create their own faux library card and include it at the front of the album. There's no right or wrong way to create a sign-in page.

After you've created your sign-in page, there's only one item left for your very own circle journal: create your own entry. You should always be the first artist to respond to your own topic. Your entry will help set the stage for your album, so make it count.

Depending on the album you've selected, you might want to decorate your album's cover as well. There are no rules for the right or wrong way to do this. Just be sure your design reflects your theme and personality.

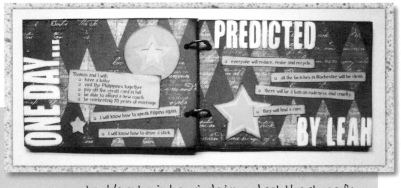

Leah's entry in her circle journal set the stage for a fabulous set of predictions from each artist.

Alecia's album is beautifully decorated and is the perfect showcase for her theme.

KEEPING THE CIRCLE GOING

After you've created your entry, it's time to pass your journal on to the next person in your group and for you to receive the next journal in line. Stick to your agreed timeline, and your own collaborative album will be back in your hands in no time at all.

Following these simple guidelines will help your circle stay happy, moving along, and working well:

- **Respect each other's art.** Don't work on someone else's scrapbook while drinking a soda, eating a burrito, or while you're infected with pinkeye. Treat their journal as your own.

- **Respect each other's time.** Often in circle journal groups there will come a time when an artist fails to meet a deadline. The best way to handle this for the group to simply stay in touch with each other so everyone is informed of the situation. Nine times out of ten, the journal is completed and back on track within a short amount of time.

- **Know when to back out.** If you're consistently behind in getting your journals completed, talk to the group about a way you can still participate without holding everyone up. Sometimes, this involves simply creating the scrapbook pages on your own and sending them directly the album's owner so she can add them later.

- **Be understanding.** People get sick, and family emergencies happen. Although circle journals are important, other things are more important. Be flexible with the members of your group and allow them to take the time they need. (Not everyone can be like Angie , who gave birth and then finished and mailed a circle journal just a few days later!)

A SAMPLING OF CIRCLE JOURNALS

There are many fantastic reasons to get involved in a circle journal project; to meet and bond with other scrapbookers or to challenge your creativity and grow artistically are just two. But perhaps the most convincing reason—and the reason circle journals are so incredibly popular right now—is the beautiful assortment of layouts that, upon the completion of the journal's travels, are yours to own.

One of the most exciting parts of this project was working with six other women who are so stylistically different from each other. Each of our journals has become a truly beautiful work of art and a real collaborative effort. See for yourself in this sampling of the best pages our circle journals hold.

BEAUTY

I selected "Beauty" as the theme for my circle journal because I am so intrigued by the things in life that add beauty to an otherwise seemingly dull world. After creating a spread on my love for modern dance, I had no idea what to expect from the other artists.

Alecia's fun layout showcases all the things and people around her that she finds beautiful.

HOMETOWNS

Angie's journal celebrated the places we currently live and all of the things we love (and don't love) about our hometowns.

Rachael's layout surprised a lot of us, as we had no idea her town was so small and unique.

Alexis created this spread about the beauty of love that was truly touching.

Michelle's beautiful beach photographs and stunning page design were a perfect match for her Florida hometown.

FAVORITE PHOTOGRAPHS

Michelle's journal was one of my favorites to work on. As scrapbookers, we place a lot of emphasis on our photos. To be able to choose any photo we wanted and create a layout about it was truly a treat.

This layout of Rachael's was instantly touching, as she shared about her experience of feeling like a true photographer for the first time.

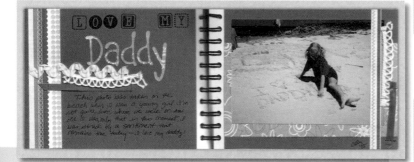

I chose to create my entry using a favorite childhood photo from the beach.

ONE DAY

Leah's album inspired all of us to think about our dreams for the future, be they silly, practical, or a little bit of both.

For my entry, I elected to reflect on a dream I share with so many women—to truly believe in myself.

SERENDIPITY

Alexis invited us to share a story of something wonderful that happened by accident.

The birth of Rachael's son Dylan was pure serendipity and made their family complete.

Angie also experienced serendipity in pregnancy by being able to unexpectedly share the birth of her daughter with her parents.

Once again, Alexis wowed us with her fantastic use of handwriting and artistic flair.

MY FIVE SENSES

Rachael invited each of us to create a layout about the things that most tickle our five senses. This was definitely a fun journal to work on!

Leah wowed everyone with this phenomenal look at how scrapbooking stimulates her senses.

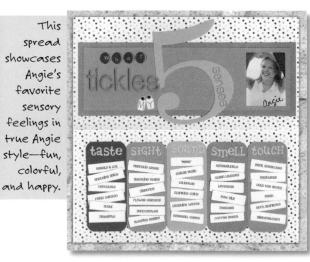

This spread showcases Angie's favorite sensory feelings in true Angie style—fun, colorful, and happy.

GAL PALS

Alecia asked us to celebrate the women in our lives who mean the most to us. We happily obliged.

Alecia's tribute to the women in her life was a truly powerful way to kick off her album celebrating female friendships.

Michelle's layout about friends united in a common goal was inspiring to read and simply beautiful to look at.

THE LEAST YOU NEED TO KNOW

- Circle journals are a fun and unique way to connect with a group of fellow scrapbook artists.

- There's no wrong way to create a circle journal. Each participant chooses her own theme and design scheme.

- Respect the other members of your circle journal group to keep things moving along smoothly.

- Participating in a collaborative project results in a final album unique from any other that you own.

IN THIS CHAPTER:

- Using your scrapbooking supplies to create beautiful all-occasion gift cards

- Understanding the basics of card design

Your kindness blesses me

Chapter **18**

Beyond the Page: Greeting Cards

People have been exchanging greeting cards for centuries. In today's fast-paced, e-mail-driven society, there's just something special about receiving a card in the mail. Even when it's simply a store-bought standard greeting card, an excited feeling occurs as you open the envelope—simply because you know someone is thinking of you.

When you take the time to make a card for someone special, you're going above and beyond the call of duty. Not only will your recipient be happy and touched that you took the time to remember him or her, but you took the time to make the card yourself. Imagine just how much more special that is.

CARD DESIGN BASICS

Card design is much like scrapbook design. The canvas is smaller and the elements are fewer, but ultimately, the same design principles you learned in Chapter 2 can be applied to greeting card design.

For many people, cardmaking is a hobby all by itself—most often paired with rubber stamping. I won't dive into advanced cardmaking techniques here—these designs have been kept simple and easy and have been designed to help you quickly and easily create some fantastic cards. To explore card making in further detail, check out Appendix E for some fantastic resources.

If you get stuck when designing a card, simply look back to earlier chapters and apply what you've already learned. Most of the scrapbooking techniques I've covered can be transferred to cardmaking.

SIZE REALLY DOES MATTER

You can make handmade cards in all sorts of creative shapes and sizes, but the most common size for handmade cards is 5½×4¼ inches. This size is perfect for creating your own cards for two key reasons.

First, a single sheet of 8½×11-inch cardstock yields exactly two cards of this size. Simply cut your sheet in half. Then fold each piece in half, and you now have the foundation for two separate cards.

Also, cards of this size fit perfectly in A2 invitation envelopes, which are widely available at your local stationery or mass merchant store. Many times, it can be difficult to find an envelope to fit your handmade card. Using this standard card size can help alleviate that problem.

UNDERSTANDING DESIGN

Like the design of a scrapbook page, the design of a card can also be broken down into sketch form. Once again, this allows you to view the card design in its simplest form and use it for additional projects. Consider this card:

This card is bold and fun but to a novice card maker, it might appear intimidating to create.

After careful examination, it's easy to see how the design fits together:

The card's basic design is simpler to understand when presented in sketch form.

When you understand the basic design of cards, it becomes easier to adapt designs to your own liking and style. Keep these principles in mind when working on the projects in this chapter and while designing your own cards.

BIRTHDAY CARDS

For children, the birthday celebration is the highlight of each year. As we grow older, however, many adults begin to feel negatively about the aging process and might not take as much delight in the day. Even so, birthdays are definitely worth celebrating. By giving a handmade birthday card, you are showing the recipient that you truly care, and that you are simply delighted he or she is in your life.

BOLD AND BEAUTIFUL BIRTHDAY CARD

This fun card design works well for any birthday. It's simple and bold, creating a festive look for any recipient. Best of all, you can create this card in just a few minutes, making it an ideal choice for last-minute cards.

This striking card is the perfect fit for a special man in your life.

To create this card, you'll need the following supplies:

- **8½×5½-inch piece of cardstock (Scrapworks)**
- **Coordinating patterned paper scraps (Scrapworks)**
- **Birthday Rubber Multi-Stamp (EK Success)**
- **Black ink pad**

To make your card, follow these steps:

1. **Fold the cardstock sheet in half.**
2. **Attach the patterned paper scraps to the top and bottom of the card, cutting to size if necessary.**
3. **Use the rubber stamp to add the greeting to the card.**

PAPER CUTS

Note that Multi-Stamps by EK Success contain several greetings in one stamp. Be sure the saying you want is selected before you apply ink.

Remember that greeting cards work well when catered to the recipient. Don't be afraid to change the design to accommodate the person you're choosing to honor.

By changing the colors and saying, this card design takes on a whole new look.

STRIPES OF COLOR CARD

This card is another fun and easy choice for birthdays. Its strong geometric design adds to its overall appeal. This card is a great choice for teens, as the stripes and bold design will likely appeal to younger recipients.

To create this card, you'll need the following supplies:

- 8½×5½-inch piece of white cardstock (Bazzill Basics), plus an additional scrap of cardstock at least 1½-inch square

- Coordinating patterned paper scraps (American Crafts)

- 1⅛-inch circle punch (Whale of a Punch by EK Success) or other circle cutting system

- Happy Birthday foam stamp (Image Tree by EK Success)

- Black ink pad

To make your card, follow these steps:

1. **Fold the cardstock sheet in half.**

2. **Cut your patterned paper scraps into strips, varying size and length.**

3. **Adhere scraps to card, alternating designs.**

4. **Use the rubber stamp to add the greeting to your cardstock scrap.**

5. **Using the circle punch, cut a circle around the stamped greeting.**

6. **Adhere the circle to the front of the card.**

PICTURE THIS

Try this card design with all sorts of patterned paper combinations—it's a great way to use up any scraps you have on hand.

HAPPY BIRTHDAY CARD WITH RIBBON

This fun card is great for kids and adults alike. It's easy to make and leaves a fantastic final impression with your recipient.

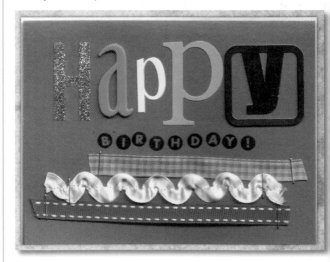

To create this card, you'll need the following supplies:

- 8½x5½-inch piece of blue cardstock
- Letter stickers (Me & My Big Ideas, Arctic Frog, Heidi Grace Designs)
- Plastic letter (Heidi Swapp)
- Metal letter clip (Scrapworks)
- Alphabet rubber stamp set (PSX distributed by Inkadinkado)
- Black ink pad
- 3 small ribbon scraps (Creative Impressions, Venus Industries)
- Stapler

To make your card, follow these steps:

1. **Fold the cardstock sheet in half.**
2. **Adhere alphabet letters spelling "Happy" across the top of the card.**
3. **Stamp the word "Birthday!" underneath.**
4. **Attach ribbon scraps horizontally under greeting using stapler.**

No matter which designs you choose, your handmade cards are sure to be a hit at the next birthday party you attend. For even more fun, try color-coordinating your card designs to match your wrapped gifts.

THANK YOU CARDS

Because it's so essential to express appreciation for those who have made a special effort to add joy to your life, thank you cards are perhaps the most important cards we send. Since I was a young girl, my mother has ingrained it in my head that every time I receive a gift, it's incredibly important to send out a note of thanks. I'll admit that as an adult, I'm not always as timely about this as I should be. Even so, I try to take the time to send a handmade thank you whenever I can. It's always nice when someone thinks of me, and it's very important to me that I express my gratitude whenever I can.

PICTURE THIS

Handmade thank you cards make great gifts. Consider producing several copies of your favorite design. Then, pair each with an envelope, stack them up, and tie them with a wide ribbon.

STAMPED FLORAL CARD

This feminine card is perfect for a friend or family member. Consider sending it as an extra-special thank you for a shared kindness.

Your kindness blesses me

The beautiful shades of pink and gray on this card create a truly stunning effect.

To create this card, you'll need the following supplies:

- 8½x5½-inch sheet of patterned paper (Daisy D's)
- "Your Kindness Blesses Me" rubber stamp (Wordsworth)
- Paper flowers (Prima)
- White cardstock scrap
- Corner rounder punch
- Black ink pad

To make this card, follow these steps:

1. Fold the patterned paper sheet in half.
2. Stamp the greeting on the scrap of white cardstock and then cut it out.
3. Use the corner rounder punch to round the corner edges of the cardstock.
4. Attach the cardstock piece to the bottom right corner of the card.
5. Attach the paper flowers to the card.

EMBOSSED DAISY PATCH CARD

This card is truly elegant. It might take a little more time to complete than some of the other cards you've done so far, but the end results are worth it. The embossed detail on this card is so beautiful. When you send this card, your recipient will know you are truly thankful.

Use the Spellbinders Wizard die-cutting and embossing system to create this gorgeous card.

To create this card, you'll need the following supplies:

- 8½x4½-inch sheet of green cardstock
- Scrap pieces of yellow and purple cardstock
- Wizard die-cutting and embossing system, Daisy Patch Die, Excalibur Alphabet Die Set (Spellbinders)
- White ink pad

To make this card, follow these steps:

1. Using the Wizard, cut and emboss the Daisy Patch shape from yellow cardstock. Note that the die contains a complete frame, so be sure to cut the entire shape.
2. Trim away any excess paper from the shape's edges.
3. Using the die as a stencil, apply white ink to the raised areas of the image.
4. Fold the cardstock sheet in half. Adhere the Daisy Patch image to the cardstock.
5. Cut and emboss the phrase *Thank You* from purple cardstock.
6. Adhere the letters to the card in the frame opening.

PAPER **C**UTS

Note that the Embossed Daisy Patch Card is not the same size as the others you're creating in this chapter. Be sure to use an appropriately sized envelope when sending this card.

BEAUTY QUEEN THANK YOU

A perfect choice for your best friend, this card says "thanks" in style. Its fun design is perfect for any feminine birthday.

To create this card, you'll need the following supplies:

- **8½×5 ½-inch piece of pale purple cardstock**
- **Pink dotted self-sticking mesh (Magic Mesh)**
- **3 small paper flowers (Prima)**
- **Chipboard beauty queen (Etcetera by Provo Craft)**
- **Black pen**

To make your card, follow these steps:

1. **Fold the cardstock sheet in half.**
2. **Tear the ends of a length of mesh to create an uneven edge.**
3. **Adhere the mesh to the card.**
4. **Glue the chipboard queen to the card.**
5. **Glue the paper flowers to the card.**
6. **Using a black pen, write "Thanks!" in the top-right corner of the card.**

Again, saying "thank you" is one of the most important things you can do. Whether you're thanking someone yourself or creating a pile of cards for gift-giving, these designs are sure to please.

CARDS FOR EVERY DAY

Sometimes, you just want to say hello. Perhaps a friend of yours moved away recently or is taking a long vacation. Maybe your favorite sibling lives far away. Or maybe you just want to send a card to your next-door neighbor, letting her know how much she means to you. Whatever the occasion, the greeting cards in this section let a special person know you're thinking of him or her.

A FUN HELLO

This card is bold and inviting; it clearly communicates your message. Full of texture and easy to create, try sending this card next time you need a simple way to say "hello."

This fun card features quite a bit of texture, adding to its appeal.

To create this card, you'll need the following supplies:

- **8½×5 ½-inch sheet of patterned paper (BasicGrey)**
- **Patterned paper scrap (BasicGrey)**
- **Squeeze hand tool, Floral die set, Olivia alphabet set, Sparkle texture embossing die (QuicKutz)**

To make this card, follow these steps:

1. **Fold the patterned paper sheet in half.**
2. **Attach the patterned paper scrap to the center of the card, cutting to size if necessary.**
3. **Cut the floral shapes using the QuicKutz system. If desired, add texture with the sparkle embossing die. Adhere the shapes to the top of the card.**
4. **Cut the letters using the Squeeze hand tool. Adhere these to the bottom of the card.**

PICTURE THIS

One of the most popular times of year for sending cards is during the holiday season. Any of the card designs in this chapter can be used to create beautiful holiday greeting cards. Simply substitute the papers and products used for holiday-themed items.

JUST BECAUSE

Sometimes, you need your greeting cards to have a classy look. Try this simple design. Created in just three simple steps, the timeless beauty of this card will last much longer than the time it takes you to create it. Perfect for that special "thinking of you" moment, send this card next time you need to let someone know you truly care.

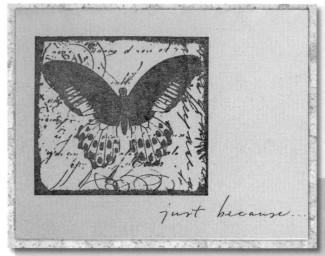

This stunning card is made beautiful by creating it from iridescent paper.

To create this card, you'll need the following supplies:

- **8½×5 ½-inch sheet of iridescent patterned paper (Polar Bear Press)**
- **Butterfly rubber stamp (Stampington & Company)**
- **"Just Because" rub-on phrase (Wordsworth)**
- **Black ink pad**

To make this card, follow these steps:

1. **Fold the paper in half.**
2. **Stamp the butterfly on the left half of the card.**
3. **Add the rub-on word to the bottom right corner of the card.**

DREAM

This beautiful card can be used for any occasion. Whether you simply need a note card that's blank inside, or you want to encourage a special friend to follow her heart after graduation, this card is a great choice.

To create this card, you'll need the following supplies:

- 8½×5 ½-inch-inch piece of white cardstock
- 5½×4½-inch piece of music print patterned paper (Life's Journey by K&Company)
- 5½×3-inch piece of dictionary print vellum paper (Life's Journey by K&Company)
- Scrap of chipboard at least 3 inches square
- Altered letter images (Crafty Secrets)
- Angel vintage image (Artchix Studio)
- Slide-mount die and cutting system (Sizzix)
- Cream-colored paint (Heidi Swapp)

To make your card, follow these steps:

1. **Fold the cardstock sheet in half.**

2. **Adhere the music print paper to front of the card.**

3. **Tear the edge of the vellum to create a soft finish.**

4. **Adhere the vellum to the card along the left edge.**

5. **Adhere the altered letter images spelling "Dream" on the vellum.**

6. **Using the Sizzix system, cut a slide mount from the chipboard.**

7. **Paint the slide mount with cream paint, and set aside to dry.**

8. **When dry, carefully peel away some of the paint to create a distressed look.**

9. **Adhere the angel image to the slide mount so the image shows through the window.**

10. **Adhere the slide mount to the card.**

Regardless of the occasion, sending handmade greeting cards is a great way to let someone know you are thinking of him or her. These beautiful designs help you achieve the perfect tone when creating your cards. Remember to have fun making your cards, and be sure to write a special message inside to make the card even more meaningful.

THE LEAST YOU NEED TO KNOW

 Creating and sending handmade cards is a fun and rewarding experience.

 Working with a standard card size can help you conserve paper and makes it easy to find the right size envelopes.

 Card design is similar to scrapbook design. Follow the basics, and you can't go wrong.

 Try giving a set of handmade cards as a gift.

IN THIS CHAPTER:

- Using your scrapbook supplies to create beautiful décor items for your home

- Dressing up your desk with a custom photo frame

- Creating unique magnets and calendars, fun for the kitchen or a school locker

- Decking the walls with scrapbook-y projects

play. **adventure**. fun.
SWING. SLIDE. CLIMB.
Walk. Jump. Run.

play is home...

Sunday	Monday	Tuesday	Wednesday	Thursday	Friday	Satu
1	2	3	4	5	6	
8	9	10	11	12	13	
15	16	17	18	19	20	
22	23	24	25	26	27	
29	30					

Chapter 19

Covering Your Halls and Walls: Scrapbook Décor

By now, you probably think you've created all you can. After countless albums, several greeting cards, and a few unique projects, it feels like there's nothing new left to create.

This couldn't be further from the truth. Now it's time to tackle the surfaces of your home. Whether it's a calendar for your wall, magnets for your refrigerator, or a framed masterpiece for your living room, you can create many different types of projects to enhance your living space. Photographs and scrapbook art were meant to be shared—try your hand at creating an item to display year-round.

FOR YOUR DESK: A CLIPBOARD PHOTO FRAME

Framed photographs have been a staple in the gift-giving world for as long as I can remember. Every Father's Day, it seems, kids nationwide take a photograph of themselves, pop it into a frame, and happily offer it as the perfect gift. Why not take the idea of desktop art one step further and create a true work of art? This project is a perfect gift—although you probably won't want to part with it.

This colorful project is quick and easy and makes a beautiful addition to your home.

This photo frame project is quick and easy, but you'd never know it from the finished product. All you need is about an hour, a favorite 4×6-inch photo, and a few basic supplies:

- **5×7-inch black clipboard photo frame (7gypsies)**
- **Patterned paper (Scrapworks)**
- **Chipboard letters (Heidi Swapp)**
- **Paper flowers (Prima)**
- **Rhinestones**
- **Assorted ribbon scraps (Creative Impressions, Making Memories, May Arts)**
- **White cardstock scrap**
- **Computer or black pen**

To create this project, follow these simple steps:

1. **Mount your photo on patterned paper. Feel free to layer several different designs, as I did. I also swiped a black ink pad across the edge of each piece to create contrast.**

2. **Place your mounted photograph under the glass in the frame. Tighten the screws to secure.**

3. **Add the chipboard letters across the top of the glass. (Note: only the bottom half of each letter is mounted on the glass.) Add a rhinestone to any letter you want.**

4. **Adhere paper flowers to the bottom right corner of the frame. Add rhinestones to the flower centers.**

5. **Using your computer or a black pen, write a caption on a piece of black cardstock. Slide the cardstock into the label holder on the far right edge of the frame.**

6. **Knot ribbon scraps around the hole on the clip.**

That's all there is to it! Six simple steps and you have now created a beautiful piece of framed art that will make the perfect gift or addition to your home.

FOR YOUR KITCHEN

The kitchen is the center of activity in many homes. It's not just a place where families gather to cook and eat meals. In my home, it's also the place where you can find the calendar, make a phone call, and pick up the mail. The projects in this section are designed to make your kitchen (or any other room) feel just a little more like home.

FIVE-MINUTE PHOTO MAGNETS

This project is one of the easiest you'll ever do, and it's also one of the most fun. I first discovered how to make these magnets when I discovered the *Xyron machine.*

SCRAP SPEAK

The **Xyron machine** is a machine designed to both laminate items as well as provide a full, even adhesive coating to items. It can also be used to apply a magnetic backing to items.

Xyron machines come in many sizes and styles, and cartridges are available for each model. These cartridges determine what the machine can do at any given time. Some cartridges provide two-sided lamination, lamination on the top of an item and adhesive on the bottom, or simply place adhesive on the bottom of a die cut to create a sticker. Many specialty cartridges are available as well. For this project, we'll be using the magnet cartridge.

The Xyron 510 is a great introductory model with many uses, perfect for beginning to intermediate crafters.

Like many people, I keep my refrigerator covered in photographs. The problem I was encountering is that my photos kept falling down whenever I'd open or shut the fridge. The magnets I was using weren't strong enough to hold the weight of all the photographs. Enter these quick and easy 5-minute magnets.

Photo magnets are fast and easy and add a unique touch to your refrigerator door.

To create a magnet, all you need are these supplies:

- **A 4×6-inch photo of your choice**
- **Xyron machine loaded with Laminate/Magnet cartridge**
- **Sticker accents (Bazzill Basics)**
- **Corner rounder punch**

PICTURE THIS

These magnets are a great project for teens, who love to make them for the inside of their school lockers.

To make a magnet, simply follow these steps:

1. **Use the corner rounder punch to round the corners of your photo.**
2. **Attach a sticker of your choice to the photograph, leaving a bit hanging off the edge if desired.**
3. **Run the photo through the Xyron machine according to the manufacturer's directions.**
4. **Trim away any excess magnet.**

Done! I love that my photos no longer fall off my refrigerator, plus I've added a touch of fun to them as well.

PICTURE THIS

You can use a Xyron machine to make a magnet out of just about anything! Try printing copies of your completed scrapbook pages at 4×4 inches and then make them into refrigerator magnets for those you love.

TWELVE-MONTH WALL CALENDAR

Everyone needs a calendar. Or at least, everyone I know does. If you've learned to live life without one, please fill me in on your secret! Creating your own calendar can take a bit of time, but it's quite a bit of fun, and you'll end up with a project you can enjoy all year long.

To create your calendar, you'll first need to select 12 photographs you'd like to include, one for each month of the year. Print these out at 5×7 inches so they'll really stand out on your calendar pages.

This calendar is ready for use and looks great hanging in your kitchen or home office

After you've selected your photos, you're ready to gather up your supplies and get started. You'll need the following supplies:

- **Blank calendar (Pinecone Press)**
- **Patterned paper and coordinating stickers for each month of the year (Reminisce)**
- **Textured cardstock to match your patterned paper selections (Bazzill Basics)**
- **QuickKutz hand tool and Studio alphabet set, or letter stickers of your choice**
- **Black ink pad**
- **Black pen**

Selecting seasonal photos is part of the fun of this project, such as this photograph for October.

Start creating your calendar by first designing the top page for each month of the year:

1. **Attach a full sheet of patterned paper to the blank side of the calendar page.**

2. **Mount your chosen photograph onto the cardstock.**

3. **Rub the top of a black ink pad around the edge of the cardstock to provide contrast.**

4. **Mount your photo onto the patterned paper.**

5. **Finish off your design with stickers and additional accents.**

You might want to add a small amount of ribbon or other elements to your pages, but be sure you do this sparingly. The calendar pages should be primarily flat. If your pages are too bulky, it will be hard to write on the calendar when you need to. Plus, if your pages are too heavy, the calendar will strain under the weight and won't hang well.

The patterned paper collections designed by Reminisce are perfect for this project because of their built-in design, which allows you to achieve beautiful pages without too much bulk.

After you've designed all your calendar tops, you'll need to fill in the bottom of your calendar pages. Start by die cutting each month's name using cardstock scraps from your layout designs. If you don't want to use a die-cutting system, letter stickers or handwriting will make a fine substitute.

Your final step is to fill in the days of each month. You can use rubber stamps or stickers to do this, but I opted to simply use a black pen.

PAPER CUTS

Be careful when filling in the dates on your calendar. Be sure you start on the correct day of the week, and note how many days are present in each month.

This calendar top for August is perfect. The rickrack used is very lightweight, adding as little bulk as possible.

FOR YOUR WALLS

Last but not least, it's time to dress up the walls of your home. These two projects are perfect for any room in the house.

8×8-INCH WALL HANGING

This wall hanging project can be completed in a matter of hours and provides a charming addition to any room.

A wall hanging is the perfect accent for your home décor.

To prepare to create this project, simply select a favorite photo or two, each printed no larger than 5×7 inches. Then, round up the following supplies:

- **8×8-inch Picture It scrapbook page frame (Picture It)**

- **Patterned paper (Chatterbox)**

- **Paper flowers (Prima)**

- **Foam alphabet stamp set and paint (Making Memories)**

- **Rub-on letters (Heidi Grace Designs)**

- **Ribbon (May Arts)**

Creating your wall hanging is simple and easy. Follow these quick steps:

1. **Cut your patterned paper to 8×8 inches.**

2. **Adhere your photographs to the paper.**

3. **Insert your paper into the frame.**

4. **Attach flowers to the top right corner of the frame.**

5. **Stamp your title in the bottom left corner of the frame, adding rub-on letters if desired.**

6. **Wrap ribbon around the frame, and tie a bow. This both secures your paper in place and provides a decorative accent.**

7. **Tie a length of ribbon and thread behind the frame for easy hanging.**

PAPER CUTS

When stamping on plastic with paint, be sure to allow plenty of time for the paint to dry. It's best to let it sit overnight. For faster drying time, lightly sand the plastic before you begin stamping.

ALTERED CLIPBOARD

These days, more and more scrapbookers are turning to the world of office supplies for inspiration. From the clipboard desktop frame we made earlier to this larger project, scrapbookers everywhere are proving that office supplies are hardly boring.

This altered clipboard project is a beautiful accent piece for your office or for use any room in your home.

Begin by choosing several photographs for your altered clipboard. I recommend printing at least one at 5×7 inches, although the choice is up to you. Next, be sure you have all the necessary supplies:

- **12×12-inch white hanging clipboard (Melissa Frances)**

- **Acrylic paint in Cream, Cotton Candy, and Sea (Heidi Swapp)**

- **Instant Decoupage Glue/Sealer/Finish in Matte (Aleene's)**

- **Patterned paper (BasicGrey)**

- **Rubber stamps (Stampington & Company)**

- **Rub-on letters (Creative Imaginations)**

- **Ribbon (May Arts)**

- **Paper flowers (Making Memories)**

- **Black ink pad**

PAPER CUTS

This project can take quite a bit of time, primarily because many steps require ample drying time before moving on to the next step. Be sure you allot yourself enough time to complete it.

When you have your supplies, you're ready to begin:

1. Paint your entire clipboard surface, including edges, Cream. Let this dry.

2. Using a sponge, add Cotton Candy paint to surface. Let this dry.

3. Repeat step 2 using Sea paint.

4. Adhere a sheet of patterned paper to the clipboard. If you like, apply Sea paint to bottom edge of paper and let dry.

5. Using black ink, stamp images onto the paper. Let this dry.

At this point, your clipboard should look something like this.

6. Add your photographs, arranging them as you like.

7. Use rub-on letters to add a title to your clipboard.

8. Using a foam brush, apply Instant Decoupage over all the elements on your clipboard, including the photographs. This seals them in place and protects them from harm. Be sure to smooth out any air bubbles that might form. Let this dry.

After sealing, your clipboard is ready for the final touches.

9. Wrap ribbon around top of clipboard, securing it on the back side with heavy-duty tape.

10. Add a flower using a strong adhesive.

Your clipboard is now complete. This beautiful item is sure to be a treasure for quite a long time.

THE LEAST YOU NEED TO KNOW

- Desktop frames are easy to create and make wonderful gifts.

- Refrigerator magnets are a fast and easy project and are also well suited for children and teenagers.

- Creating a custom wall calendar can be an enjoyable activity that will bring you a full year of pleasure.

- Wall hangings and altered clipboards featuring your favorite photographs are beautiful additions to your décor and office.

Appendix A

Scrap Speak Glossary

3-ring albums   One of the most versatile albums on the market today. Completed pages are placed in page protectors, which are then stored in the album's ring system. 8½×11-inch office binders make an affordable choice for the scrapper on the budget. Three-ring albums are not expandable.

ABC album   An album with one page for each letter of the alphabet, usually related to a specific theme or event.

accent or **embellishment**   A predesigned add-on for a scrapbook page, often taking the form of a sticker or die-cut shape.

accordion album   A scrapbook made of a single length of paper, folded multiple times in opposite directions to create several panels, which serve as the pages of the album.

Bay Box album   A specialty scrapbook album produced by Scrapworks. Featuring divided page protectors designed for 4×6-inch photographs, this album system is ideal for individuals who want to create a scrapbook but have limited time or resources to devote to page design.

chipboard   A cheap, stiff, paper board made from discarded paper, usually used as backing material in packaging.

collage   A composition of several papers and/or materials, pasted or glued together to create a new and different artistic effect.

cropping   The act of trimming photographs and papers to the desired size for a project.

distressing   The act of making a new element appear old by crinkling, sanding, or inking.

dry adhesive   An adhesive that's dry to the touch yet tacky. It does not run and is applied like a tape. It sets immediately upon application. Dry adhesive is best for adhering paper to paper.

focal point   The strongest element on a scrapbook page, and the place on the page to which your eye is naturally drawn.

journaling   On a scrapbook page, this is the block of text that includes descriptive information about the photographs on the page.

layout sketch   A layout map indicating the placement of photographs, journaling, and other page elements.

mat A decorative border that surrounds a photograph, providing it with a framelike base to set it apart from the rest of the scrapbook page.

post-bound album A scrapbook that's bound using a system of posts and screws. Completed pages are placed in page protectors. Post-bound albums are expandable and are generally considered the most attractive type of album.

rub-on transfer images Letters or images that appear on a sheet of translucent specialty paper. When this paper is placed over another sheet of paper and rubbed firmly, the image transfers to the new paper without leaving a seam or any additional marks.

scrapbooking The act of taking photographs and combining them with specialty papers, accents, and journaling to create a customized photograph album.

spiral-bound album An album that is much like an everyday school notebook, consisting of several blank pages bound together into a single album. These albums are not expandable and do not include page protectors.

theme scrapbooking An approach to scrapbooking that focuses on relationships, events, and emotions with equal emphasis. Pages are created and displayed in a specific order, not necessarily chronologically.

traditional scrapbooking A method of scrapbooking in which pages are created and displayed in chronological order, generally with one page devoted to each major event occurring in a calendar year.

wet adhesive A liquid-based adhesive that requires additional time to dry before it is set. Wet adhesive is best for applying other materials— metal, plastic, and wood, for example —directly to paper.

Xyron machine A machine designed to both laminate and provide a full, even adhesive coating to items. It can also be used to apply a magnetic backing to items.

Appendix **B**

Album Design Worksheets

When you set out to begin a scrapbook album project, sometimes it can feel a bit overwhelming. You've got a stack of photographs, a pile of products, and a set of instructions. But how do you get from here to a completed album? One step at a time.

These album design worksheets can help you plan each of your album projects. Use them to track your photographs, journaling, and any additional elements you plan to include in your albums.

Vacation Album Planning Worksheet (Chapter 4)

Your Vacation Destination: _____

Divide your pile of photographs into groups of two to four photos per event or moment you want to capture in your album. Record the results here.

Event/Moment	Photographs	Possible Page Title/Journaling

ADDITIONAL THOUGHTS/NOTES

_____

_____

_____

_____

Holiday Album Planning Worksheet (Chapter 5)

For this project, select two or more photographs for each holiday you want to include.

Holiday	Photographs (Years Taken)
New Year's Day	_____
Valentine's Day	_____
St. Patrick's Day	_____
Independence Day	_____
Easter	_____
Passover	_____
Halloween	_____
Thanksgiving	_____
Chanukah	_____
Christmas	_____
Kwanzaa	_____
_____	_____
_____	_____
_____	_____
_____	_____
_____	_____
_____	_____
_____	_____
_____	_____

ADDITIONAL THOUGHTS/NOTES

_____

_____

_____

_____

_____

ABC Album Planning Worksheet (Chapter 6)

Begin by selecting a title theme for each letter of the alphabet. Then, be sure you have a photograph to match.

Title   **Photograph**

A: _____   _____
B: _____   _____
C: _____   _____
D: _____   _____
E: _____   _____
F: _____   _____
G: _____   _____
H: _____   _____
I: _____   _____
J: _____   _____
K: _____   _____
L: _____   _____
M: _____   _____
N: _____   _____
O: _____   _____
P: _____   _____
Q: _____   _____
R: _____   _____
S: _____   _____
T: _____   _____
U: _____   _____
V: _____   _____
W: _____   _____
X: _____   _____
Y: _____   _____
Z: _____   _____

ADDITIONAL THOUGHTS/NOTES

_____
_____
_____
_____

School Days Album Planning Worksheet (Chapter 7)

Sort your school photos into categories based on the type of photographs you want to include in your album. Make note of how many photos you have in each category and include details and/or journaling notes when you record your photographs.

Photos   **Photographs**

☐ New Year's Day   _____

☐ Field trips   _____

☐ Outdoor events   _____

☐ Recognitions and events   _____

☐ Daily life in the school routine   _____

☐ Favorite activities   _____

☐ Time with friends   _____

☐ Seasonal and holiday parties   _____

☐ Photos with your child's teacher   _____

☐ Miscellaneous fun photographs and head shots   _____

☐ School portraits   _____

☐ Send digital camera to school with student   _____

☐ _____   _____

☐ _____   _____

☐ _____   _____

☐ _____   _____

☐ _____   _____

ADDITIONAL THOUGHTS/NOTES

_____

_____

_____

_____

_____

Musical Mini-Album Planning Worksheet (Chapter 9)

Follow the steps in Chapter 9 to plan your album project. Use this worksheet to plan the framework for your song selections.

	Song Title and Artist Name	Photographs to Match
1.		
2.		
3.		
4.		
5.		
6.		
7.		
8.		
9.		
10.		
11.		
12.		
13.		
14.		
15.		

ADDITIONAL THOUGHTS/NOTES

Lessons Learned Album Planning Worksheet (Chapter 10)

Subject of Album: _____

Lessons I have learned from this person:

1. _____
2. _____
3. _____
4. _____
5. _____
6. _____
7. _____
8. _____
9. _____
10. _____

Photographs and/or memorabilia I can include in this album:

1. _____
2. _____
3. _____
4. _____
5. _____
6. _____
7. _____
8. _____
9. _____
10. _____

ADDITIONAL THOUGHTS/NOTES

_____
_____
_____
_____
_____

Friends Are Forever Album Planning Worksheet (Chapter 11)

Subject of Album: _____

Fill in your journaling for each album section:

1. Remember the Time _____

_____

_____

2. Favorite Moments _____

_____

_____

3. I Never Told You _____

_____

_____

4. Funniest Memories _____

_____

_____

5. I Admire You Because _____

_____

_____

Now, write a letter to your friend. You can later copy this into your album:

_____

_____

_____

_____

_____

ADDITIONAL THOUGHTS/NOTES

_____

_____

_____

_____

All-About-Me Album Planning Worksheet (Chapter 12)

Fill in these quick lists to help you get started on your album's creation.

My Roles

1. _____
2. _____
3. _____
4. _____
5. _____

6. _____
7. _____
8. _____
9. _____
10. _____

My Comforts

1. _____
2. _____
3. _____
4. _____
5. _____

6. _____
7. _____
8. _____
9. _____
10. _____

My Dreams

1. _____
2. _____
3. _____
4. _____
5. _____

6. _____
7. _____
8. _____
9. _____
10. _____

My Beliefs

1. _____
2. _____
3. _____
4. _____
5. _____

6. _____
7. _____
8. _____
9. _____
10. _____

ADDITIONAL THOUGHTS/NOTES

_____

_____

_____

_____

_____

All-About-Me Album Planning Worksheet (Chapter 12) *continued*

My Obsessions

1. _____
2. _____
3. _____
4. _____
5. _____

6. _____
7. _____
8. _____
9. _____
10. _____

My Fears

1. _____
2. _____
3. _____
4. _____
5. _____

6. _____
7. _____
8. _____
9. _____
10. _____

My Talents

1. _____
2. _____
3. _____
4. _____
5. _____

6. _____
7. _____
8. _____
9. _____
10. _____

My Collections

1. _____
2. _____
3. _____
4. _____
5. _____

6. _____
7. _____
8. _____
9. _____
10. _____

ADDITIONAL THOUGHTS/NOTES

_____
_____
_____
_____
_____

All-About-Me Album Planning Worksheet (Chapter 12) *continued*

My Hobbies

1. _____   6. _____
2. _____   7. _____
3. _____   8. _____
4. _____   9. _____
5. _____   10. _____

Other: _____

1. _____   6. _____
2. _____   7. _____
3. _____   8. _____
4. _____   9. _____
5. _____   10. _____

Other: _____

1. _____   6. _____
2. _____   7. _____
3. _____   8. _____
4. _____   9. _____
5. _____   10. _____

Other: _____

1. _____   6. _____
2. _____   7. _____
3. _____   8. _____
4. _____   9. _____
5. _____   10. _____

ADDITIONAL THOUGHTS/NOTES

_____
_____
_____
_____
_____

Recipe Album Planning Worksheet (Chapter 13)

Use this worksheet to choose the categories you want to include in your recipe album (5 maximum):

- ▣ Appetizers
- ▣ Soups and Salads
- ▣ Entrées/Main Dishes
- ▣ Miscellaneous

- ▣ Beverages
- ▣ Side Dishes
- ▣ Beef

- ▣ Vegetarian
- ▣ Desserts
- ▣ Cookies

- ▣ Pasta
- ▣ Cakes and Candy
- ▣ Poultry and Fish

Category: _____

Recipes:

1._____
2._____
3._____
4._____
5._____
6._____

7._____
8._____
9._____
10._____
11._____
12._____

Category: _____

Recipes:

1._____
2._____
3._____
4._____
5._____
6._____

7._____
8._____
9._____
10._____
11._____
12._____

ADDITIONAL THOUGHTS/NOTES

_____

_____

_____

_____

_____

Recipe Album Planning Worksheet (Chapter 13) *continued*

Category: _____

Recipes:

1._____   7._____

2._____   8._____

3._____   9._____

4._____   10._____

5._____   11._____

6._____   12._____

Category: _____

Recipes:

1._____   7._____

2._____   8._____

3._____   9._____

4._____   10._____

5._____   11._____

6._____   12._____

Category: _____

Recipes:

1._____   7._____

2._____   8._____

3._____   9._____

4._____   10._____

5._____   11._____

6._____   12._____

What's Next Album Planning Worksheet (Chapter 15)

What do you wish for? In your wildest dreams (both realistic and far-fetched), what do you want to accomplish in your life? Create a list of your future dreams here and then select at least eight of them to feature in your album.

ADDITIONAL THOUGHTS/NOTES

Appendix C

Materials Guide

This materials guide lets you know exactly what products were used to create each of the scrapbook pages featured in this book. (See the appropriate chapter text for the materials used to create each album project.) Use the manufacturer listings in Appendix D to find any products you're looking for.

If no specific brand name is listed, any brand of that product will work fine. In most cases, if you can't locate the exact item you're looking for, substituting a similar product will still produce fantastic results.

CHAPTER 1

Merry
Textured cardstock and chipboard square (Bazzill Basics), die-cut letters (Paige Mini by QuicKutz), foam alphabet stamps and paint (Making Memories), ribbon (Creative Impressions), decorative staples (Fastenator by EK Success).

Memories of Santa
Patterned paper (Daisy D's), decorative tape (Heidi Swapp), rickrack (Artchix Studio), metal accent (JoAnn Scrapbook Essentials), yarn, ribbon, staple, vintage postcard.

Whatcha Lookin' At
Patterned paper (KI Memories, Rob and Bob Studio by Provo Craft), cardstock (Making Memories), alphabet stickers (Doodlebug, American Crafts), brads (Doodlebug), computer font.

Katie
Cardstock, pens (Zig Writer by EK Success).

Drive My Car
Cardstock, patterned paper (KI Memories), chipboard letters (L'il Davis Designs).

CHAPTER 2

Fine Art
Cardstock (Bazzill Basics, Prism), photo corners, button, flower, lanyard, and chipboard alphabet (Heidi Swapp).

Anna's Baptism
All products by Anna Griffin.

Exactly One
Rub-on letters (Making Memories), frame, border, and floral accents (Tim Coffey for K&Company), cardstock, patterned paper, braided thread.

According To
Cardstock (Bazzill Basics), patterned paper (7gypsies), black tile letters (Westrim Crafts), stencil letters, tags, rub-ons, brads, and date stamp (Making Memories), metal letters (JoAnn Scrap Essentials, Pressed Petals), computer fonts (Creating Keepsakes).

Sarah's Happy Little Life
Cardstock, patterned paper (Scrapworks), and Arial and Arial Narrow computer fonts.

CHAPTER 2 *continued*

Xmas 1983
Patterned paper (Chatterbox), cardstock (Bazzill Basics), chipboard letters (Making Memories), die-cut letters (Katie by QuicKutz), ribbon (May Arts), computer font (Creating Keepsakes), foam alphabet stamps, paint.

Always Laugh
Patterned paper (Christina Cole by Provo Craft), rub-ons, acrylic paint (Making Memories), label holder (7gypsies), ribbon (Creative Impressions, Rusty Pickle, Offray), brads.

New
Patterned paper (Heidi Grace Designs), rub-on letters (Gin-X by Imagination Project).

A Sacred Moment
Patterned paper, tag, rub-on letters (KI Memories), ribbon (May Arts), stapler.

This Is Me
Patterned cardstock, metal letters (Making Memories), ribbon (American Crafts), computer font (CK Curly Cursive by Creating Keepsakes), journaling background (Creating Keepsakes Creative Clips)

CHAPTER 3

All About Me
Patterned paper (All My Memories), die-cut letters (Indulgence by Spellbinders for the Wizard), brads, clips, and ribbon (Creative Impressions), paper flowers (Prima), clear letters (Scrapworks), leaves, lace, blue glitter.

Real Love
Patterned paper (BasicGrey), rubber stamp (Wordsworth), loop braid trim (Wrights).

James and Mommy
Patterned paper (BasicGrey), copper brads (Creative Impressions), die-cut letters, tag shape, and ocean shapes (Spellbinders for the Wizard), cardstock (Bazzill Basics), page jewelry (Mermaid Tears), green and blue glitter, coastal netting, bottle caps, clear finish.

Remember This Forever
Cardstock (Bazzill Basics), patterned paper (Paper Adventures, Bo Bunny Press), metal frame (Making Memories), heart brads (Frills by Queen & Company), dimensional accents (Jolee's by EK Success), ribbon (Offray, May Arts, Creative Impressions, Carolee's Creations), rub-ons (Making Memories, Bo Bunny Press).

Through a Child's Eyes
Cardstock (Bazzill Basics), stickers (American Crafts), Century Gothic computer font.

My Rocky
Patterned paper (SEI), letters and vintage images (Crafty Secrets), rickrack trim (Making Memories), chipboard label holder and strips (Heidi Swapp).

Everyday Love
Cardstock, patterned paper, tag die cut, quote sticker, metal clip (Scrapworks), letter stickers (Wordsworth), Pharmacy and Century Gothic computer fonts, thread.

Friends
Patterned paper (NRN Designs), cardstock (Bazzill Basics), ribbon (Wrights), Black Dymo Label Maker Tape, flowers (Prima), Deckle Tag Punch (EK Success), pink alcohol color wash dye, glitter.

31
Foam stamps, paint, rub-ons, slide letters (Making Memories), file folder (Rusty Pickle), ribbon (Wrights), nail heads, ribbon slide, jeweled flower, page jewelry (Mermaid Tears).

Woman of Wisdom
Patterned paper (Anna Griffin), chipboard letters (Pressed Petals), chipboard diamonds (Heidi Swapp), die-cut letters (Paige Mini by QuicKutz), paint, cardstock.

Birthday Girl
Patterned paper (Provo Craft), plastic letters (Heidi Swapp).

CHAPTER 3 *continued*

More Cheese
Patterned paper, metal frame, fabric tab, circle accent and sticker (Scrapworks), flower, rub-on letters, iron-on letters (Heidi Swapp), ribbon (Creative Impressions, May Arts), metal photo corners (Making Memories).

CHAPTER 4

Professional Beach Family
Cardstock (Bazzill Basics), Century Gothic computer font.

Relax
Patterned paper (Me and My Big Ideas), letter stickers (American Crafts), Century Gothic computer font, dragonfly accent (EK Success).

Timeless Beauty
Cardstock (Bazzill Basics), patterned paper (K&Company), date stamp, rub-on letters (Making Memories), Book Antiqua computer font.

Lost Island
All products by Karen Foster Design.

Space Needle
Cardstock (Bazzill Basics), patterned paper (KI Memories, Sweetwater), snaps (Making Memories), Space Pontiff and Century Gothic computer fonts, transparency.

Kayaking
Cardstock (Bazzill Basics), patterned paper, circle tags (KI Memories), 2Peas Typo computer font (TwoPeasinaBucket.com).

Fun at Dow Gardens
Patterned paper, stickers (BasicGrey), ribbon (May Arts), flowers (Prima), brads (Doodlebug).

CHAPTER 5

Birthday Balloons
Cardstock (Bazzill Basics), circle foam stamp (Heidi Swapp), gems, acrylic paint (Making Memories), ribbon (American Crafts), die-cut letters (Abigail by QuicKutz).

Holiday Hoopla
Die-cut letters (Wishblade), cardstock, eyelets.

I'm Cute, and I Ain't Lion
Patterned paper (Frances Meyer, Karen Foster Design, Doodlebug Design, Provo Craft), stamps (Hero Arts, Making Memories), ribbon (Offray), ribbon charm, photo corners (Making Memories).

Love Day
Patterned paper (Urban Lily), alphabet stickers (American Crafts), die-cut letters (Boxed Brush by Sizzix), ribbon (Offray), SP Pretty Purkey computer font.

Coloring Eggs
Cardstock (Bazzill Basics), patterned paper, alphabet stickers, tag (BasicGrey), brad.

Popcorn Balls
Cardstock (Bazzill Basics), patterned paper (The Paper Loft), Typeset computer font, circle punches.

Chanukah 2004
Cardstock (Bazzill Basics), patterned paper (Chatterbox, KI Memories), die-cut letters (Sophie by QuicKutz), die-cut shapes (QuicKutz).

2004 Christmas Tree
Cardstock (Bazzill Basics), patterned paper (Memories Complete), ribbon (Fibers by the Yard), rubber stamps (Stamped in Ink).

Make a Wish
Cardstock (Bazzill Basics), all other supplies by KI Memories.

CHAPTER 6

Wonder
Cardstock (Bazzill Basics), patterned paper (Reminisce), metal letters (Making Memories).

New
Patterned paper (Heidi Grace Designs), rub-on letters (Gin-X by Imagination Project).

Pickle
Cardstock (Bazzill Basics), patterned paper (Reminisce), rub-on letters, metal clip letter (Scrapworks).

Very Special
Cardstock (Bazzill Basics), patterned paper (SEI), letter stickers (Me and My Big Ideas).

Halloween
Patterned paper, stickers (Karen Foster Design), rub-on letter (Scrapworks), metal tag.

Anna
Patterned paper (K&Company), letter stickers (Creative Imaginations).

Quiet
Patterned paper, dimensional letters (K&Company), ribbon (Offray).

Reading
Patterned paper (Gin-X by Imagination Project), rub-on letters (Making Memories), metal-edged canvas tag (Creative Imaginations).

A Is for Anna
Patterned paper (Karen Foster Design), computer font (Creating Keepsakes).

Chris 3 Weeks
Patterned paper (BasicGrey), ribbon (May Arts), twill (Creative Impressions), acrylic paint, foam stamps, brads (Making Memories), photo corners (Pioneer), cork accents (Lazer Letterz), rub-ons (Making Memories, Li'l Davis Designs), epoxy words (Creative Imaginations), letter stickers (Provo Craft), stamps (Hero Arts), shipping tag.

The Naming of Olivia
Cardstock (Bazzill Basics), patterned paper (K&Company), metal charm letters, flower brads, cloth pocket, staples, rub-on letters, date stamp (Making Memories), die-cut letters (Lollipop by Sizzix), Trots Light computer font.

Aquarius
Patterned paper (Making Memories), cardstock (Bazzill Basics), 2Peas High Tide computer font (TwoPeasinaBucket.Com), American Typewriter computer font, rickrack.

In the Year 1979
Patterned paper (Sweetwater), letter stickers (Mrs. Grossman's, Wordsworth), 1979 Year Sheet (CKC Creations), eyelets (Making Memories), photo corners (Xyron).

First Swim
Patterned paper (Flair Designs), letter cards (Bazzill Basics), ribbon (Venus Industries, May Arts, Offray), flowers (Prima).

Re:fresh
Cardstock (Bazzill Basics), patterned paper (My Mind's Eye), Century Gothic computer font, hole punch.

Baby Buddies
Patterned paper, letter stickers (BasicGrey), stickers (7gypsies), rub-on stitches (My Mind's Eye).

I See
Patterned paper (Karen Foster Design), ribbon (Offray), printed twill (Carolee's Creations), buttons (Dress It Up), rub-ons, charm (Making Memories), Times New Roman computer font.

Anna, Things I Wish to Tell You
Patterned paper (Heidi Grace Designs), foam stamps, paint (Making Memories), ribbon (May Arts, Offray), Maiandra GD computer font.

CHAPTER 7

Madison, the Sixth-Grade Science Expert
Patterned paper, rub-ons, accents (Scrapworks, Rusty Pickle, 7gypsies, Creative Imaginations, Li'l Davis Designs).

Back2School
Cardstock (Bazzill Basics), circle punch, circle cutter, Wishblade cutting system, Proxima Sans, Billy, Book Antiqua, Arial Black, and Abadi MT Condensed computer fonts.

First Field Trip
Cardstock (Bazzill Basics), patterned paper (Scenic Route Paper Company), cardstock sticker (Flair Designs), fiber (Fibers by the Yard), staples, rub-ons, brads (Making Memories), Cupcake and Arial computer fonts, small chalkboard accent.

Reach High
Cardstock (Bazzill Basics), patterned paper (KI Memories, Anna Griffin), rub-ons (Making Memories), Headline Two computer font.

DHS Homecoming Dance
Patterned paper (Doodlebug Designs), chipboard coaster (Li'l Davis Designs), ribbon (American Crafts), foam stamps, paint (Making Memories), corner rounder (EK Success), paper clip, note cards, small file folder.

Grad
Cardstock (Bazzill Basics), patterned paper (Chatterbox), chipboard letters (Heidi Swapp), cardstock stickers (Doodlebug Design), photo turns (Making Memories), ribbon (May Arts).

CHAPTER 8

84
Patterned paper (Karen Foster Design), die-cut letters (Studio by QuicKutz), cardstock.

Always in Motion
Cardstock (Bazzill Basics), patterned paper, quote, monograms (KI Memories), rub-on letters (Doodlebug Design), yellow frame accent (Scrapworks).

Rugby
Patterned paper, stickers (Fiber Scraps), alphabet stickers (Mustard Moon), tinting ink (Fiber Scraps), chipboard letters, rub-ons (Making Memories), alphabet squares (Junkitz), bottle cap, chipboard letters (Li'l Davis Designs), rub-ons (7gypsies).

Legacy
Patterned paper (Captured Elements), stamps (Hero Arts), office supply tags.

Fearless
Cardstock (Bazzill Basics), patterned paper (Chatterbox), rub-on letters, tag (Making Memories).

Card Sharks
Cardstock, patterned paper (Scrapworks), chipboard letters (Heidi Swapp).

How to Hula Hoop
Cardstock (Bazzill Basics), patterned paper (American Crafts), computer fonts, handcrafted chipboard circles, green brads.

CHAPTER 9

Dream Come True
Patterned paper (Karen Foster Design), denim eyelet trim (Wrights), woven label (Me & My Big Ideas), monogram letter (Bazzill Basics).

The Cake
Patterned paper (Wordsworth), eyelet letters, eyelets, brads (Making Memories), mini frames (KI Memories), flowers (Prima), pink mulberry paper, transparency, ribbon.

CHAPTER 9 *continued*

Now THAT'S a Kiss
Patterned paper (KI Memories), cardstock (Bazzill Basics), photo corners (Heidi Swapp), ribbon, charm (Making Memories), stickers, rub-ons (Doodlebug Design), clay letters (Li'l Davis Designs), Parade computer font.

Together
Cardstock (Bazzill Basics), patterned paper (Chatterbox), tag (Scrapworks), kraft paper.

You're Never Too Old to Swing
Stickers (Doodlebug Design), cardstock, 2Peas Tasklist computer font (TwoPeasinaBucket.Com), Arial Narrow computer font.

Faves
Patterned paper (Gin-X by Imagination Project), foam stamps, paint (Heidi Swapp), Dymo label maker, white cardstock scraps, thread.

CHAPTER 10

Because of You
Cardstock (Bazzill Basics), patterned paper (Junkitz, Christina Cole by Provo Craft), dimensional sticker (Christina Cole by Provo Craft), Snap-Ease (Rob & Bob Studio by Provo Craft), ribbon, letter stickers (American Crafts), Problem Secretary Normal computer font.

Thankful for Grandparents
Cardstock (Li'l Davis Designs, Making Memories), patterned paper (Li'l Davis Designs), die-cut letters (Boxed Brush by Sizzix), ribbon (KI Memories), metal accents (Making Memories), Century Gothic and Tahoma computer fonts.

Mom's House
Cardstock (The Crafter's Workshop, Bazzill Basics), patterned paper (The Crafter's Workshop), stickers (The Paper Loft, SEI), Century Gothic computer font, fibers, chalk.

The Man I Call Dad
Cardstock (Bazzill Basics), patterned paper (Life's Journey by K&Company), elements (Daisy D's), book cloth (Chatterbox), wood shape, paint, transparency, walnut ink, Bookman Old Style, CK Cursive (Creating Keepsakes), Balzac, Rage Italic LET computer fonts.

Mom
Patterned paper, quote (Karen Foster Design), cardstock (Bazzill Basics), ribbon (Making Memories), Typeface Tints (The Designer's Library), typewriter key letters (K&Company), CK Fable computer font (Creating Keepsakes).

Portrait of Marsha
Cardstock (Bazzill Basics), patterned paper (Melissa Frances, K&Company, Anna Griffin), CluKennedySH computer font.

Depth of Life
Cardstock (Bazzill Basics), patterned paper, tacks (Chatterbox), quote (Karen Foster Design), Dymo label maker.

CHAPTER 11

Fun Friends
All products by Gin-X, Imagination Project.

Gas Garden Girls
Cardstock (Bazzill Basics), patterned paper (BasicGrey), date stamp (Making Memories), alphabet charms, ribbon.

Basketball Mom Friends
Patterned paper, tag, alphabet stickers, monogram (BasicGrey), CK Chemistry (Creating Keepsakes) and 2Peas Pricecheck (TwoPeasinaBucket.Com) computer fonts, brad.

I Scream U Scream
Stickers (KI Memories, American Crafts), rub-ons (SEI), Dymo label maker, ribbon, buttons, cardstock.

Catitude
Patterned paper (Carolee's Creations), rub-ons, accents (American Crafts, Making Memories), cardstock (Bazzill Basics).

CHAPTER 12

My Life in the Nineties
Photo corners (Heidi Swapp), all other products by Scrapworks.

My Life at 25
Cardstock (Bazzill Basics), stickers (KI Memories), rub-ons, foam stamps (Making Memories), ribbon (May Arts, Offray).

Proud to Be Ally
Patterned paper (Leaving Prints, Gin-X by Imagination Project), chipboard letters (Making Memories), rickrack (Artchix Studio), computer fonts.

I Am Me
Cardstock (Bazzill Basics), patterned paper (Making Memories), stencil letter (Ma Vinci's Reliquary), Dymo label maker, ribbon (Go with the Grain, Offray, Bobbin Ribbon), foam stamps (Making Memories), rubber stamps (Stampabilities, Image Tree by EK Success, PSX distributed by Inkadinkado, Hero Arts).

I'll Bet You Didn't Know
Patterned paper (SEI), brads, word charms, flower snaps (Making Memories), stickers (Magenta), transparency film, Serrific Grunge computer font.

Genuine
Cardstock (Prism), patterned paper (BasicGrey), alphabet stickers (Gin-X by Imagination Project, Scenic Route Paper Company), alphabet stamps (Hero Arts).

Why I Wear Yellow
Patterned paper (Junkitz), rubber stamps (Ma Vinci's Reliquary), rub-on letters (Making Memories), computer font.

98 Pounds
Patterned paper (Scenic Route Paper Company), foam stamps (Making Memories), Uncletypewriter, Century Gothic, Carpenter ICG, and Punch Label computer fonts.

CHAPTER 13

Strawberries and Ice Cream
Patterned paper, letter stickers (SEI), bubble letters (KI Memories), cardstock (Bazzill Basics), 2Peas Barefoot Processor computer font (TwoPeasinaBucket.Com).

Eating Blueberries
Cardstock (Bazzill Basics), patterned paper (Rusty Pickle, My Mind's Eye), eyelets, brads, sticker (Making Memories), ribbon (May Arts), index tabs (7gypsies), transparency, hemp, date stamp, thread, American Typewriter and BlackJack computer fonts.

Truffles
Patterned paper (Chatterbox, KI Memories), foam stamps, photo corners (Making Memories).

Ice Cream
Cardstock (Bazzill Basics), patterned paper (Rusty Pickle), alphabet stickers (Arctic Frog), ribbon, Tia Flip Flop computer font.

Bake a Cake
Cardstock (Prism), patterned paper (Junkitz), charm, clip, sticker gems (American Traditional Designs), alphabet stickers (American Crafts), rubber stamps (Hero Arts), rickrack (Doodlebug Design), staples (Making Memories).

Someone's in the Kitchen
Patterned paper (KI Memories, Doodlebug Design), alphabet stickers (American Crafts, Doodlebug Design), ribbon, floss, buttons (Making Memories).

Spicy
Patterned paper (BasicGrey, Junitz), cardstock (Bazzill Basics), monogram (BasicGrey), plastic letters (Heidi Swapp), ribbon (Offray, May Arts), stickers (Scrapworks), Century Gothic computer font.

CHAPTER 14

The Magic of an Ordinary Day
Patterned paper, stickers (BasicGrey), chipboard letters, metal hinges (Making Memories), cardstock (Bazzill Basics), rhinestone flowers (Mermaid Tears), ribbon (Fibers by the Yard), flower, gemstone brads.

A Day in My Life
Patterned paper (KI Memories), cardstock (Bazzill Basics), Fulton Artist stamp, butterbrotpapier, Elegant computer fonts, brads, bottle cap, handcrafted filmstrip border.

24 Hours of Being Two
Cardstock (Bazzill Basics), brads, stickers (Sticker Studio, Chatterbox, Creative Imaginations), stamps (PSX distributed by Inkadinkado).

A Typical Day
Cardstock (Bazzill Basics), patterned paper, ribbon, stickers (Fiber Scraps), descriptive stickers, wood tag (Chatterbox), foam alphabet stamps (Making Memories), metal tag (7gypsies), bottle caps (Li'l Davis Designs), Noisebaby computer font.

April Showers Bring May Flowers
Cardstock (Bazzill Basics), trellis frame, custom cut flowers and leaves (Outrageous Daisy), rub-on letters, denim letters (Making Memories), cork alphabet stickers (Karen Foster Design), thread, brads.

CHAPTER 15

Dreaming of a Dog
Patterned paper, stickers, metal charm (Flair Designs), library pocket, tag (Outrageous Daisy), ribbon (Creative Impressions).

2005 Goals/Dreams/Hopes
Cardstock, library pockets (Bazzill Basics), patterned paper, rub-on flowers, ribbon, letter "A", icicles (KI Memories), circle clip (Li'l Davis Designs), rub-on letters (Chatterbox), Page pebbles, photo anchors (Making Memories), Missy BT and Broadway BT computer fonts.

I Believe in You
Cardstock (Bazzill Basics), ribbon (Making Memories), icicles (KI Memories), rub-ons (Li'l Davis Designs).

When I Get Older
Patterned paper (Chatterbox), cardstock (Bazzill Basics), GF Halda Normal and Century Gothic computer fonts, date stamp.

Walking in my Daddy's Shoes
Patterned paper (Scenic Route Paper Company), cardstock (Bazzill Basics), chipboard letters (Li'l Davis Designs), love worn letters (Carolee's Creations), ribbon (Offray), paint, washer words (Making Memories), foam stamps (Li'l Davis Designs), rub-ons (My Mind's Eye), buttons, fibers.

Where Will I Be One Year from Now
Patterned paper, ribbon, stickers, tags, borders (SEI), Flower (Prima), Century Gothic computer font.

CHAPTER 16

Top Dog
Patterned paper (Karen Foster Design), printed twill (Carolee's Creations), metal charm (Flair Designs).

Scrapping with Ashley
Cardstock (Scrapworks), chipboard letters (Chatterbox), flower (Heidi Swapp), letter stickers (Wordsworth), mini file folder and bookplate (Outrageous Daisy).

CHAPTER 17

Beauty
Patterned paper (7gypsies), foam alphabet stamps (Creative Imaginations), stamps (PSX distributed by Inkadinkado), chipboard beauty queen (Provo Craft).

My Hometown
Cardstock (Bazzill Basics), patterned paper (KI Memories), title letters (Xyron Wishblade), plastic letters (Heidi Swapp), tags (KI Memories), ribbon (KI Memories, May Arts).

Welcome
Patterned paper (KI Memories, 7gypsies), chipboard accents (Provo Craft), braided trim (Wrights), stamps (Nostalgiques by EK Success), foam alphabet stamps (Creative Imaginations).

Alecia's Gal Pals Circle Journal
Album (SEI Preservation Series), patterned paper (Imagination Project), canvas tag (Making Memories), rub-ons (BasicGrey), rubber stamps (Image Tree by EK Success), cardstock, buttons.

Serendipity Instructions
Cardstock (Bazzill Basics), patterned paper, border stickers (Christina Cole by Provo Craft), ribbon (Doodlebug Design), flowers (Prima), hand lettering.

Sign Me
Patterned paper, stickers (BasicGrey), Dymo label maker, flowers (Prima), twill tape (Wrights), brads.

One Day ... Predicted by Leah
Patterned paper (Scenic Route Paper Company), die-cut letters and shapes.

CHAPTER 17 *continued*

Love
Letter stickers (American Crafts), all other supplies by Scrapworks.

Beauty is in the I of the Beholder
Cardsock (Bazzill Basics), patterned paper (KI Memories), rub-ons (Doodlebug Design, SEI, KI Memories), stickers (SEI, Making Memories).

Auburn
Patterned paper (My Mind's Eye, Karen Foster Design), flowers (Prima), alphabet stickers (Scrapworks), coin envelopes (Bazzill Basics), brads (American Traditional Designs).

Home Is Where the Heart Is
Patterned paper (Gin-X by Imagination Project), rickrack (Fibers by the Yard), rub-ons (Making Memories, Rusty Pickle), Dymo label maker, ribbon, markers, transparency, clear keepsake jewel, Angelina computer font.

Lighthouse Favorite Photo
Patterned paper (American Traditional Designs, Chatterbox, KI Memories), charms (American Traditional Designs), ribbon (May Arts, Doodlebug Design).

Love My Daddy
Cardstock (Bazzill Basics), patterned paper (Chatterbox), ribbon and trims (Wrights, Venus Industries, Offray), alphabet stamps (Inspirables by EK Success).

Someday I Will Believe
Patterned paper (Karen Foster Design), metal tags (American Crafts), velvet alphabet stickers (Making Memories), clear heart shapes (Heidi Swapp).

One Day
Cardstock (Bazzill Basics), flowers (Prima), brads (Making Memories), pattered paper (KI Memories), circle punch, white pen.

Dylan
Cardstock (Bazzill Basics), patterned paper (Scenic Route Paper Company), alphabet stickers (Scenic Route Paper Company, American Crafts), epoxy alphabet (Li'l Davis Designs), printed twill (Creative Impressions), wood frame (Chatterbox), acrylic tag (Doodlebug Design), photo corner die cuts (QuicKutz), brads.

Pure Serendipity
Cardstock (Bazzill Basics), patterned paper (K&Company), paper flowers (Prima), stickers (Chatterbox).

Five Senses of Scrapbooking
Patterned paper (BasicGrey, KI Memories), flower punch (EK Success), game board letters (Making Memories), GoodGirl computer font, alphabet beads, acrylic jewels.

What Tickles My 5 Senses
Cardstock (Bazzill Basics), patterned paper (Me and My Big Ideas), die-cut letters (Olivia by QuicKutz), additional die cutting (Xyron Wishblade), stickers (EK Success, Doodlebug Design), plastic letters (Heidi Swapp), Too Much Paper computer font.

Friends Who Share a Dream
Patterned paper, stickers (BasicGrey), flowers (Prima), loopy brads (Karen Foster Design), Supernderz (Junkitz), brads (Creaive Imaginations), glitter, photo corners, vellum, Fine Hand computer font.

Gal Pals
Patterned paper (Imagination Project), paper flower (Prima), snap (Rob & Bob Studio by Provo Craft), cardstock.

Roll Call
Patterned paper (Flair Designs), flowers (Prima), library pocket, die-cut shapes.

CHAPTER 18

Thanks
All products by Scrapworks.

Appendix D

Internet Resources

The Internet offers a wealth of information, advice, and products for today's scrapbook artist. Want to find a particular product? Got a question about a technique? Need help figuring out the perfect touch for a layout you're working on? Help is now just a click away. From downloadable products to creativity challenges, you'll be sure to find whatever you need online.

MANUFACTURER LISTINGS

Love one of the products you've seen used in this book? This listing of websites directs you to the manufacturer of many of the products mentioned in this book so you can find more information about the product as well as purchasing information.

7gypsies
www.sevengypsies.com

Anna Griffin
www.annagriffin.com

Arctic Frog
www.arcticfrog.com

BasicGrey
www.basicgrey.com

Bazzill Basics
www.bazzillbasics.com

Chatterbox, Inc.
www.chatterboxinc.com

Crafty Secrets
www.craftysecrets.com

Creative Impressions
www.creativeimpressions.com

Daisy D's Paper Company
www.daisydspaper.com

Duncan Enterprises
www.duncancrafts.com

EK Success
www.eksuccess.com

Flair Designs
www.flairdesignsinc.com

Heidi Swapp
www.heidiswapp.com

Junkitz
www.junkitz.com

Karen Foster Design
www.karenfosterdesign.com

KI Memories
www.kimemories.com

Making Memories
www.makingmemories.com

Melissa Frances
www.melissafrances.com

O'Scrap!
www.oscrap.com

Outrageous Daisy
www.outrageousdaisy.com

Provo Craft
www.provocraft.com

Sizzix
www.sizzix.com

QuicKutz
www.quickutz.com

Scrapworks
www.scrapworks.com

Spellbinders
www.spellbinders.us

Stampington & Company
www.stampington.com

Venus Industries
www.venusindustries.com

Wordsworth
www.wordsworthstamps.com

Wrights
www.wrights.com

Xyron
www.xyron.com

COMMUNITY SITES

These websites offer a place for scrapbook artists to gather and share ideas. They are free to join. You'll find message boards and extensive layout galleries at each one. These sites often feature regular contests and challenges for members, and many offer an online store of their very own.

Cropper's Cottage
www.cropperscottage.com

Scrap Talk
www.scraptalk.com

Scrapbook.com
www.scrapbook.com

Scrapjazz
www.scrapjazz.com

Scrappers Anonymous
www.scrappersanonymous.com

Two Peas in a Bucket
www.twopeasinabucket.com

ONLINE STORES

Don't have a local scrapbooking store? Your worries are over. Check out some of these great online stores to find the products you want at affordable prices.

Addicted to Rubber Stamps
www.addictedtorubberstamps.com

Addicted to Scrapbooking
www.addictedtoscrapbooking.com

Busy Bee Scrapbooking
busybeescrapbooking.com

CardsNStamps
www.cardsnstamps.com

A Cherry On Top
www.acherryontop.com

Creative Xpress
www.creativexpress.com

Down Memory Lane Company
www.downmemorylaneco.com

Lifetime Moments
www.lifetimemoments.com

Luv2Scrapbook
www.luv2scrapbook.com

Memory Villa
www.memoryvilla.com

A Million Little Things
www.amillionlittlethings.com

Paper Addict
www.paperaddict.com

Scrapbook Hut
www.scrapbookhut.com

ScrapGal
www.scrapgal.com

Stampington & Company
www.stampington.com

MAGAZINES

Magazines can be a fantastic source of up-to-date information and inspiration. Both in print and online, these publications help keep you informed of the latest scrapbooking trends and techniques.

Creating Keepsakes
www.creatingkeepsakes.com

Digital Scrapbooking Magazine
www.digitalscrapbooking.com

Legacy
www.stampington.com/html/legacy.html

Memory Makers
www.memorymakersmagazine.com

Paper Crafts
www.papercraftsmag.com

PaperWorks
www.paperworksmagazine.com

Scrap & Stamp Arts
scottpublications.com/ssa

Scrapbook Answers
www.scrapbookanswers.com

MAGAZINES *continued*

Scrapbook Trends
www.scrapbooktrendsmag.com

Scrapbooking.Com Magazine
www.scrapbooking.com

Scrapbooks Etc. by *Better Homes & Gardens*
www.bhgscrapbooksetc.com

Simple Scrapbooks
www.simplescrapbooksmag.com

DIGITAL SCRAPBOOKING AIDS

For the computer-savvy scrapbooker, these sites feature downloadable papers and accent designs—everything you need to create fantastic pages. You'll also find tutorials and instruction on how to use your computer to create digital scrapbook pages.

DigiScrapZ
www.digiscrapz.com

Do It Digi
www.doitdigi.com

Pixel-Expressions
www.pixel-expressions.com

Promos4Digiscrappers
www.promos4digiscrappers.com

Scrap Girls
www.scrapgirls.com

Scrapbook-Bytes
www.scrapbook-bytes.com

Scrapbook-Elements
www.scrapbook-elements.com

Shabby Elements
www.shabbyelements.com

CAREER OPPORTUNITIES

These sites are perfect for those wishing to learn how to get their scrapbook art published in magazines and books, or those wishing to start a business selling their own supplies. No matter what your scrapbook dream, these sites can help turn it into reality.

Fun Facts Publishing
www.funfactspublishing.com

National Scrabooking Association
www.nsa.gs

ScrapSubmit
www.scrapsubmit.com

Recommended Reading

Anderson, Kelli, Alison Beachem, Jenni Bowlin, Dawn Brookey, Ali Edwards, Nichol Magourik, Tracy Miller, Faye Morrow Bell, Maya Opavska, Vanessa Reyes, Karen Russell, Julie Scattaregia, Tracie Smith, Heidi Stepanova, Loni Stevens, Sara Tumpane, and Jamie Waters. *Full Circle.* Mesa: Li'l Davis Designs, 2004.

Ball, Kimberly, ed. *The Complete Guide to Creating Heritage Scrapbooks.* Denver: Memory Makers Books, 2002.

Banker, Susan M. *Scrapbooking with Recipes: Ideas for Preserving Kitchen Memories.* Des Moines: Better Homes and Gardens Books, 2003.

Bearnson, Lisa. *Scrapbooking with Lisa Bearnson, Book 2.* Palm Coast: Primedia, 2005.

Cornell, April. *Designer Scrapbooks with April Cornell.* New York: Sterling Publishing Co., 2005.

Downey, Donna. *Photo Décor.* Bluffdale: Primedia, 2005.

Eads, Alison. *The Artful Card.* Cincinnati: North Light Books, 2005.

Edwards, Ali. *A Designer's Eye for Scrapbooking.* New York: Primedia, 2004.Ghumm, Erikia, and Pamela Frye Hauer. *Montage Memories: Creating Altered Scrapbook Pages.* Denver: Memory Makers Books, 2004.

Giallongo, Rachael, and Melissa Reynolds. *The Office Book.* Santa Ana: Pinecone Press, 2005.

Gibbons, Leeza. *Scrapbooking Traditions.* Des Moines: Meredith Books, 2005.

Haglund, Jill. *Artists Creating With Photos.* Sarasota: TweetyJill Publications, 2005.

———. *Creating Vintage Cards.* Sarasota: TweetyJill Publications, 2005.

Now that you've mastered the basics of scrapbooking, you're probably looking to expand your knowledge even further. Take a look at some of the books listed here to learn more advanced techniques or to explore some of this book's themes in greater detail.

Julian, Stacy. *The Big Picture: Scrapbook your Life and a Whole Lot More.* Bluffdale: Primedia, 2005.

———. *Simple Scrapbooks.* Bluffdale: Creating Keepsakes Books, 2000.

Kofford, Jennifer. *Ribbonrie.* Centerville: Making Memories, 2005.

Pederson, Angie. *The Book of Me: A Guide to Scrapbooking About Yourself.* Cincinnati: North Light Books, 2002.

Ross, Melody. *What to Write to Make Meaningful Albums.* Eagle: Chatterbox, 2004.

Rueger, Lydia, ed. *Creative Stamping for Scrapbookers.* Denver: Memory Makers Books, 2005.

Sower, Rebecca. *Scrapbooking Life's Little Moments.* New York: Primedia, 2004.

Tenney, Erin. *Small Collections.* Santa Ana: Pinecone Press, 2004.

White, Tracy. *The Journaler's Handbook: Everyone Has a Story.* New York: Primedia, 2004.

Willis, Tania. *Circle Journals.* Santa Ana: Pinecone Press, 2005.

Zielske, Cathy. *Clean and Simple Scrapbooking.* New York: Primedia, 2004.